POSTCARDS FROM THE E|

REMOTE BRITISH LIGHTHOUSES IN VINTAGE POSTCARDS

The Bell Rock Lighthouse · Scotland.

CHRISTOPHER NICHOLSON

Whittles Publishing

Plymouth, Smeaton Tower

Whittles Publishing

Published by Whittles Publishing Limited

Dunbeath, Caithness, KW6 6EY, Scotland

www.whittlespublishing.com

ISBN: 978-1904445-59-3

Cover and text layout by Mark Mechan

Printed and bound in Singapore by Craft Print International Ltd

CONTENTS

Above: A party of visitors to Round Island lighthouse in the Scilly Isles have made their way from the landing stage towards the lighthouse. The men are dressed in smart tweed jackets and hats which suggest that this could be a Sunday outing. Even though the island was completely devoid of any other building, or shelter, this particular light was a popular destination for such trips. The man leading the procession with a small child in hand has a white cap on indicating that he is probably one of the keepers.

ACKNOWLEDGEMENTS

Compiling this book has been a long and fascinating hunt through many private collections, lighthouse authority archives, postcard and antiques fairs, and internet auction sites to unearth some of the treasures that appear in the following pages.

To find some of these cards I've met or spoken with a large number of postcard collectors and lighthouse enthusiasts who have been only too willing to show me their collections and even trusted me to borrow some of the priceless contents for scanning. In many cases it was difficult to know what to leave behind. Without the help and patience of the following people, this book would probably never have been published; Chris Foulds, Keith Hall, Brian Chilton, Derrick Jackson, Barry Hawkins, Eddie Dishon, Mike Millichamp and Patrick Tubby.

I must also mention Lorna Hunter and Ian Webster at the Northern Lighthouse Board, and Vikki Gilson at Trinity House for their unfailing help when I was trying to track down a card of some far-flung island light, and Gerry Douglas-Sherwood, the archivist of the Association of Lighthouse Keepers (ALK) who turned up some real gems.

I should also emphasise that every image in this book has come from an actual postcard. Not a postcard-sized photograph, but an actual printed postcard that was published and sold, some of them over a century ago. Sometimes the cards are indeed actual photographs, sometimes an artist's drawing or painting. Some of them have been through our postal system and bear stamps, while others have never been postally used. But they have all been bought by someone as a postcard and have some or all of the characteristics associated with a postcard – the divided back, the square space for the stamp, the publisher's details, and the location of the image.

What I hope has resulted from all this research is not just a book of old postcards, but a document of true social history – permanent records of architectural masterpieces, the men who built and looked after them through storm and tempest, snapshots of the past and moments in time from the very edge of Britain.

Christopher Nicholson
November 2009

Beachy Head Light House. EASTBOURNE.

THE LOCATIONS OF THE LIGHTHOUSES FEATURED IN THIS BOOK

30. SULE SKERRY
31. FLANNAN ISLES
32. MONACH ISLES
33. BARRA HEAD
34. HYSKEIR
35. SKERRYVORE
36. DUBH ARTACH
37. SKERVUILE
38. SANDA
39. PLADDA
40. AILSA CRAIG
41. CHICKEN ROCK
42. WYRE
43. NEW BRIGHTON
44. TRYWN DU
45. THE SKERRIES
46. BARDSEY ISLAND
47. ST. TUDWAL'S

13. COQUET
14. INNER FARNE
15. LONGSTONE
16. BASS ROCK
17. FIDRA
18. INCHKEITH
19. ISLE OF MAY
20. BELL ROCK
21. RATTRAY HEAD
22. PENTLAND SKERRIES
23. STROMA
24. AUSKERRY
25. START POINT
26. FAIR ISLE SOUTH
27. FAIR ISLE NORTH
28. OUT SKERRIES
29. MUCKLE FLUGGA

1. BISHOP ROCK
2. ROUND ISLAND
3. LONGSHIPS
4. WOLF ROCK
5. EDDYSTONE
6. LES HANOIS
7. LA CORBIÈRE
8. PLATTE FOUGÈRE
9. CASQUETS
10. NEEDLES
11. NAB TOWER
12. BEACHY HEAD

48. SOUTH BISHOP
49. THE SMALLS
50. SKOKHOLM
51. WHITFORD POINT
52. FLATHOLM
53. LUNDY NORTH
54. LUNDY ORIGINAL
55. LUNDY SOUTH
56. GODREVY

1 PILLAR LIGHTS

Eddystone Light House Plymouth.

Pillar rock lighthouses epitomise our traditional view of a lighthouse – magnificent towers of granite rising from a sea-washed reef miles from the nearest land. They were built over a century ago by men of vision and determination – with names like Douglass and Stevenson – and manned by a special breed of keepers. They were lonely, cramped outposts of Britain subjected to ferocious assault by wind and waves. Despite their remoteness, they were an incredibly popular subject for postcards, and a vast number of them were produced featuring all the major British pillar lighthouses. For most people, their only view of such feats of engineering would be in a postcard. Sadly, they no longer have their keepers, but their warning flashes are as reliable as ever.

Above: The ugly teeth of the Eddystone reef seem to encircle the present lighthouse and the stump of Smeaton's tower. The writer of this card, which was posted to Adelaide in Australia in July 1904, has declared "Hope to sail out here tomorrow" – but not this close one hopes.

BISHOP ROCK

Bishop Rock lighthouse rises from the westernmost reef of the Scilly Isles. The present tower is the third structure to have been placed here – the first, designed by James Walker, was swept away in a gale in 1850 before it was operational, and a second tower of 1858 built by James and Nicholas Douglass proved inadequate under the onslaught of fearful Atlantic storms. It was in service for less than 30 years and is actually encased inside the present 1887 tower when it was raised and strengthened.

At 160ft, this lighthouse tower is certainly the tallest in Britain and probably the most exposed. To the west are over 3,000 miles of uninterrupted Atlantic Ocean, which smash against it with a force difficult to comprehend unless you are inside when it is shaking and shuddering. Wave pressures of up to 7,000lbs per sq ft have been recorded here – powerful enough to split granite blocks and tear a 5 cwt fog bell from its mountings on the lantern gallery.

The present Bishop Rock lighthouse was built between 1883–87 by William Douglass to the designs of his father, James Douglass – an almost identical copy of his newest Eddystone lighthouse of 1882. With precision stonemasonry it was built around the second tower, completely enveloping it without a single night of its warning flash being lost. It's the first sight of Britain that trans-Atlantic passengers on the great liners would get after leaving America, and it became the unofficial end of the 2,949 mile Blue Riband race from New York. What these passengers probably wouldn't realise is that, according to the *Guinness Book of World Records*, Bishop Rock is the world's smallest island with a building on it! The relief of the keepers here – when it was still done by boat – became a popular tourist attraction.

Position:	Western Rocks, 4 mls W of Scilly Isles
Constructed:	1883–87
Designer:	James Douglass
Builder:	William Douglass
Tower height:	160ft (49m)
Light character:	W Gp Fl (2) ev 15 secs
Range:	24 mls
Fog warning:	Horn (2) ev 90 secs
Helideck:	1976
Automated:	December 1992

The Bishop Light House, Scilly.   Gibson. Penzance.

Far left: A spectacular aerial shot of Bishop Rock lighthouse rising from a swirl of white water. The white lantern used to house one of the largest optics in the Trinity House service – an 11 ton giant which gave its flash a range of 29 miles. Today's lantern has a slightly reduced range.

Left: An earlier sepia card from 1905 with a small fishing boat, partially camouflaged by the rock itself, drifting past in calmer conditions.

LONGSHIPS

The Longships Lighthouse.   6304

Left: An interesting aerial view that shows the full extent of the Longships reef and the exposed position of William Douglass' tower on the outermost rock.

Below: An Empire View card that describes the lighthouse as "A lonely out-post". It's quite an interesting view because it was taken from inside the reef itself. We can see two of the three different landing stages, and also the considerable number of steps needed to facilitate keeper reliefs and landing of stores.

"A lonely out-post."   "Empire View"
Longships Lighthouse, Land's End.   084·10.

Longships lighthouse is only a mile from Lands End, and visible in all but the most foul conditions. It takes its name from the fact that the reef on which it stands looks a bit like a convoy of ships when viewed at sunset – hence 'long-ships'.

The first light to warn of the dangers of Longships reef was first seen in September 1795 from a short, stumpy tower designed and built by Samuel Wyatt on the Great Carnvroaz rock. At only 52ft tall it wasn't high enough and winter storms swept right over it. It was clear that another Longships lighthouse would be required.

The present tower was built by William Douglass between 1870–73. Just four months after it was lit, and before Wyatt's tower had been demolished, a huge storm in April 1874 smashed against the Longships reef and swept Wyatts redundant tower into the boiling sea below – never to be seen again.

Even though its replacement was much bigger at 114ft, it still isn't a particularly tall pillar lighthouse when compared to such giants as Bishop Rock or Skerryvore. There are some spectacular photos of this lighthouse being engulfed by winter storms.

Right: An early hand-tinted colour card from the turn of the last century showing the present Longships lighthouse on the Great Carnvroaz, the outermost and largest rock of the Longships reef. The white frame around the door was to enable semaphore flags to be read through a telescope from the keepers cottages above Sennen Cove.

The keepers here used to communicate with their families in the cottages above Sennen Cove by using semaphore flags. An area around the lighthouse door was whitewashed to ensure the two flags would stand out against the white background. Their families ashore used binoculars to 'read' the messages. Any replies were sent in the same manner.

Longships was never a popular posting for keepers. Conditions were cramped and overdue reliefs were common – even though they could often see their homes on the cliffs above Sennen. The swell and tidal surges between the teeth of the reef meant a boat relief could only be attempted in near perfect conditions, and in winter these could be far and few between. This all changed in 1979 when it was given a helideck and the relief was just a two minute helicopter flight. The last keepers left in April 1988 when it was automated, ending an unbroken run of almost 200 years of keepers on the Longships.

Left: A 1930s sepia card showing exactly how close Longships lighthouse is to the mainland. The channel between the two was often used as a shortcut for vessels rounding Lands End – like this coaster making its way from the English Channel into the Bristol Channel.

Position:	1 ml W of Lands End
Constructed:	1870–73
Designer:	William Douglass
Builder:	Michael Beazeley
Tower height:	114ft (35m)
Light character:	Iso (2) ev 10 secs W & R sectors
Range:	W18 mls, R11 mls
Fog warning:	Horn (1) ev 10 secs
Helideck:	1979
Automated:	April 1988

WOLF ROCK

Wolf Rock Lighthouse.

Such was the difficulty and uncertainty of relieving keepers at Wolf Rock lighthouse that Trinity House erected the very first helideck above a British lighthouse here in 1973. Its location, 8 miles off Lands End, in the middle of a tidal epicentre subjects it to ferocious seas and swirling currents. A calm day at Wolf Rock is a rare thing indeed – more usual were conditions similar to the ones in the card below.

The present tower was built by a combination of James, Nicholas and William Douglass between 1862–70 to the designs of James Walker. This involved the base of the tower being built in a series of 'steps' rather than being set on a circular cylinder of stone like the one at Bishop Rock. The steps were supposed to break the force of the water hitting the tower and prevent it climbing up it. There will be many former keepers who might challenge the success of this design!

To the north east of the tower a huge stone landing stage was attached, and on the end of this was a massive metal derrick pole that was rigged on relief days to pluck the new keepers from an open boat that was standing off, and dropping the retiring keepers back into it. It was, by all accounts, a pretty hair-raising experience in marginal weather. The last keepers to experience 'wet' reliefs were in 1973, and the final keepers left in March 1988 when it was automated. It has recently been converted to solar power.

Left: A calm day at Wolf Rock. This card gives us a good view of the landing stage and its metal cone, around which the landing stage was built. It could possibly be a relief day – there is the hint of a limp flag hanging from the flagpole, while to the left of the lantern there is a silhouette of a keeper waving at the approaching boat.

Position:	English Channel, 8 mls SW Lands End
Constructed:	1862–70
Designer:	James Walker
Builder:	James, Nicholas & William Douglass
Tower height:	134ft (41m)
Light character:	W Fl ev 15 secs
Range:	23 mls
Fog warning:	Horn (1) ev 30 secs
Helideck:	November 1973
Automated:	March 1988

Rough Seas and Wolf Rock Lighthouse, Land's End   PN4533

Above: Nothing out of the ordinary in this view of Wolf Rock lighthouse; waves climbing halfway up the tower and the landing stage awash with white water. Sticking out of this we can see the triangular metal cone that was an early attempt to mark the reef before the lighthouse was built, and the metal derrick pole from which the unfortunate keepers being relieved were swung from the landing stage into a pitching boat and vice versa.

LES HANOIS

The very name of this lighthouse gives us a clue that it has a French connection. It's one of the lights in the Channel Islands that is maintained by Trinity House, and bears more than a passing resemblance to two of its other pillar rocks; the Smalls and Wolf Rock.

The western seaboard of Guernsey was an absolute nightmare for shipping – a jumble of razor-sharp reefs, half-submerged ledges and rocks, and vicious swirling currents. After a campaign that lasted some 30 years, the erection of Les Hanois light in 1862 on one of the outermost rocks improved matters, but even with satellite navigation and AIS [Automatic Identification System] this is no place for the unskilled mariner.

Its history contains several notable firsts and lasts; it was the first lighthouse where the granite blocks were dovetailed vertically as well as horizontally, it was the last rock station to be automated by Trinity House and the first to be converted to solar power. It's also the most southerly of the Trinity House stations in the UK.

Like all pillar rocks, its helideck duly arrived in 1979 and its keepers departed in 1996.

132 GUERNSEY. — Hanois Lighthouse — Le Phare des Hanois . LL.

Left: A view from near Pleinmont Point that shows exactly the kind of hazards that lay in wait for unwary vessels approaching Guernsey from the west. Out of the jumble of jagged rocks and vicious reefs rises the 107ft Les Hanois lighthouse tower. It stands on a rock called Le Bisseau.

Left: One of the keepers of Les Hanois poses on the reef to the left of the tower, while another sits on the steps in front. Hanging from the lantern gallery is the original fog bell from 1862. When the station was modernised in 1964 it was removed and replaced by an electric fog horn. Compare the design of this tower and the glazing of the lantern with the lighthouse on the Smalls reef later in this book.

Position:	English Channel, reef 1½ mls W of Pleinmont Point, Guernsey
Constructed:	1861–62
Designer:	Nicholas Douglass, James Walker
Builder:	William Douglass
Tower height:	107ft (33m)
Light character:	W Gp Fl (2) ev 13 secs
Range:	20 mls
Fog warning:	Horn (2) ev 60 secs
Helideck:	1979
Automated:	January 1996

EDDYSTONE

Eddystone – the most famous lighthouse in the world – stands on a jagged reef 14 miles from Plymouth and has a history that now spans over 300 years. It's a story that encompasses the construction of five different lighthouses and all that's best in the development of lighthouse engineering; philanthropy, innovation, courage, dogged determination and skill.

The history of all five towers is too lengthy a story to even precis here, but any decent book on lighthouses* will detail the dramatic chronology of events and engineers.

Only the fourth and fifth towers can be seen today – the fifth continues its nightly vigil out on the Eddystone reef itself, where it has been for over 125 years – while its predecessor was dismantled and re-erected on Plymouth Hoe where the general public can examine John Smeaton's magnificent structure at will. Its stump remains out on the reef, but is sadly suffering much torment from winter storms.

Its design is almost identical to the present Bishop Rock light – there is just a foot difference in the height of their towers. Only the red helideck that surrounds Eddystone's lantern sets it apart from Bishop Rock's white helideck.

To mark the centenary of the present tower in 1982 it was converted to automatic operation, making it the first British pillar rock lighthouse to lose its keepers on a permanent basis. Solar power was installed in 2000 – lighthouse authorities have never been slow to make use of the technology of the era.

Position:	English Channel, 9 mls S of Rame Head
Constructed:	5 separate towers, 1698–1882
Designers:	Henry Winstanley (2), John Rudyerd, John Smeaton, James Douglass
Builders:	Henry Winstanley (2), John Rudyerd, John Smeaton, James & William Douglass
Present Tower ht:	159ft (49m)
Light character:	W Gp Fl (2) ev 10 secs
Range:	22 mls
Fog warning:	Horn (3) ev 60 secs
Helideck:	October 1980
Automated:	May 1982

Opposite page, left: An excellent artist's impression of the scene on the Eddystone reef some time after James Douglass' fifth Eddystone tower had been completed in 1882, and John Smeaton's fourth tower had been dismantled down to the level of its solid base. We can still see one of its red stripes and the dog steps leading to the entrance door. The sea conditions are fairly choppy – too choppy I would suggest for the several sailing vessels that are perilously close to the reef! Because this is the work of an artist and not a photograph, it is unlikely of course that these vessels would ever have been so close in such conditions. However, it is noticeable throughout this book that whenever a postcard carries an artist's impression, it comes with considerable artistic licence, in this case the close proximity of these vessels to obvious danger, as well as the flocks of disturbed seabirds. Look out for further examples of these in the book.

Opposite page, right: This sepia card was posted in 1925 and shows what a low tide and calm conditions were like at the Eddystone. It was calm enough for someone to actually jump onto, or sail through the reef itself to photograph it and we can see some interesting detail. All three keepers have gathered on the 'set–off' for the photograph, but have obviously been distracted by something. Lashed to the railings of the lantern gallery is the long step ladder used to clean the outside of the lantern windows. To the left is the long wooden flagpole that actually passed through the last few courses of masonry. There was a crank handle on the gallery that enabled it to be raised and a flag flown on relief days or when some of the Elder Brethren visited. To the right, the vertical structure with the curved end is the fog signal arm from where explosive charges were detonated at the end.

Plymouth. Eddystone Lighthouse in a Storm.

Plymouth. The Hoe Promenade.

Above: Another artist's impression of the Eddystone reef from a very similar viewpoint to the one opposite, that pre-dates it by several years. Smeaton's tower has not yet been dismantled and its red and white stripes are still obvious. This artist has made the sea conditions even worse, and added a clutch of galleons with no sail passing perilously close to the reef. Hanging from the gallery of the new lighthouse are two fog bells that were struck by a clockwork mechanism in times of poor visibility, and there appears to be what looks like a religious cross on the top of the new lantern. The artist has probably misinterpreted what he has seen in another card as a cross, but it's actually a weather vane.

Left: This is where John Smeaton's tower ended up – in a prime position on Plymouth Hoe looking across Plymouth Sound and out to sea to the very reef on which it stood. It is now regarded as one of Plymouth's most famous landmarks. The only part of the tower that is not genuine is the solid base – the original is still on the reef and a new base was built on the Hoe to reconstruct the tower on. In this view it still has the red and white stripes it bore out at sea, and today you can find it in exactly the same colours. However, in the intervening period it has been painted many colours since it first arrived on the Hoe – some of which would have made John Smeaton turn in his grave! Visitors can climb the 93 steps to the lantern room where a replica of the candelabra that held the 24 tallow candles Smeaton first used as his illuminant in 1759 can be viewed.

* Try *Rock Lighthouses of Britain* by Christopher Nicholson (Whittles Publishing, Caithness, Scotland ISBN 978–1904445–27–2) for a detailed and exciting history of the Eddystone lighthouses!

THE NEEDLES

The Needles showing original Lighthouse on the cliff.

Left: An artist's impression of the Needles sometime after 1859. On the cliff tops beyond, the original tower of 1786 still stands. The jagged nature of the three needles has been exaggerated somewhat!

Right: A striking view from the air showing the Needles and their lighthouse, although the helideck has yet to be added. The remains of the original tower on the cliffs no longer exist.

4938. The Needles Rocks & Lighthouse, I.W.

The Needles, as any south–coast yachtsman will tell you, are the three jagged sea stacks at the western extremity of the Isle of Wight. The story of the lighthouses here bears a striking similarity to the history of Beachy Head lighthouses further along the south coast.

An original lighthouse was built by a Mr R.Jupp in 1785 on the top of 430ft high chalk cliffs. In clear conditions it had a range of 11 miles, but often its light could not be seen through the mists and fog that formed at this height.

It was eventually abandoned and a new 101ft tower was subsequently built by James Walker in 1859 at sea level – and this is the tower that exists today. A large slice of the outermost needle had to be cut away to provide a level foundation for the stepped base, together with the accompanying cellars and storerooms.

Although it always had plenty of passing traffic, the Needles was never a popular posting for Trinity House keepers. The tower – which interestingly doesn't have the taper so commonplace with pillar rock lights – was comparatively small and conditions inside were cramped. Reliefs were done by boat from Yarmouth until it was finally fitted with a helideck in 1987, prior to its automation seven years later.

The red and white tower remains as popular as ever as a destination for tourist boats during the summer months.

Position:	English Channel, western extremity of the Isle of Wight
Constructed:	2 separate towers, 1786 &1859
Designers:	R.Jupp, James Walker
Builders:	R.Jupp, James Walker
Present Tower ht:	101ft (31m)
Light character:	W+R+G Gp Occ (2) ev 20 secs
Range:	W 17 mls, R & G14 mls
Fog warning:	Horn (2) ev 30 secs
Helideck:	1987
Automated:	December 1994

NAB TOWER

Nab Light Tower BEING TOWED FROM SHOREHAM.

MONTAGUE BLACK

CUNARD LINE   R.M.S. 'BERENGARIA'   TONNAGE 52,300

Above left: Launch day in 1920 and the Nab Tower is being towed from Shoreham into position at the entrance to Spithead. The half-finished second tower can be seen on the right, but this one was subsequently scrapped.

Above: Once settled on the sea bed it also became a pretty formidable daymark as this card shows. A Trinity House pilot vessel drifts in front of the tower while RMS *Berengaria* passes close by.

Early in 1918, attacks by German U-boats on our merchant fleet caused the Admiralty such anxiety they decided to take decisive counter measures. A daring plan was devised to sink a line of eight fort-like towers (costing £1 million each) across the Solent and to link them with steel boom nets in an attempt to close the English Channel to enemy ships.

About 3,000 civilian workmen were brought to a quiet backwater at Shoreham where work began on two of these giant towers – each 40ft in diameter with latticed steelwork surrounding the 90ft cylindrical steel tower. This rested on a hollow 80ft thick concrete base, complete with a pointed bow and stern for easy towing, that was designed to be flooded and sunk in about 20 fathoms.

One tower was complete when the war finished in November 1918, but the other half-finished giant was broken up for scrap. It was decided to use the solitary 'white elephant' to replace the old Nab lightvessel by sinking it at the eastern end of the Spithead approaches, where it would also serve as an invaluable naval defence post if required.

On a calm day in 1920 two tugs towed the tower into position. The base was slowly opened to the sea, and the brainchild of a civilian designer, Mr. G. Menzies, settled as planned and without incident, kept steady by the immense volume of water inside its base. Its large, flat top surface meant a helideck was never necessary at the Nab for relieving keepers.

Position:	English Channel/Spithead, 6 mls SE of Southsea
Constructed:	1918
Designers:	The Admiralty
Builders:	The Admiralty
Tower height:	92ft (27m)
Light character:	W Fl ev 10 secs
Range:	16 mls
Fog warning:	Horn (2) ev 30 secs
Helideck:	n/a
Automated:	May 1983

BEACHY HEAD

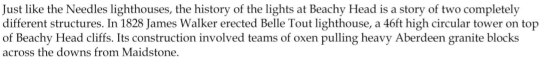

The Old Lighthouse, Beachy Head.

Beachy Head.

Just like the Needles lighthouses, the history of the lights at Beachy Head is a story of two completely different structures. In 1828 James Walker erected Belle Tout lighthouse, a 46ft high circular tower on top of Beachy Head cliffs. Its construction involved teams of oxen pulling heavy Aberdeen granite blocks across the downs from Maidstone.

Unfortunately, being on top of the highest chalk sea cliffs in Britain meant it was frequently shrouded in mist and fog and therefore an unreliable navigational aid. Not only that, the cliffs themselves were retreating at an alarming rate towards the tower – a process that still continues today. A storm in January 1999 caused thousands of tons of the cliff to fall and actually changed the shape of the coastline.

The light remained in operation until 1899 when it was abandoned. It has subsequently been a tea-room and a private house. In March 1999 it was moved back from the edge to prevent its demise as the cliffs continued to crumble. Its failure as a lighthouse has been replaced by its success as a tourist attraction.

In 1902, under the direction of Sir Thomas Matthews, the Trinity House Engineer-in-Chief, the present 142ft pillar rock tower was completed. Sited about 530ft seawards from the base of the cliffs, it took two years to complete and involved building a coffer-dam and a cableway from the top of the cliffs to carry materials down to the site. Over 3,660 tons of Cornish granite were used in its construction.

Only 3 miles from the seaside resort of Eastbourne, it is one of Britain's most photographed lighthouses.

Opposite page, far left: A lovely sepia card of Belle Tout lighthouse taken sometime after 1902 as there is clearly no lens inside the lantern room. By now the new tower down at sea level was in operation. However, this shot still shows the lighthouse in its original position. It wasn't until 1999 that the retreating cliff edge forced its owners to move the whole 850 ton lighthouse on a pioneering system of hydraulic jacks and 'float pads' some 55ft inland to prevent its disappearance over the cliffs for another half century or so.

Opposite page, right: An excellent view of the 500ft chalk cliffs at Beachy Head showing James Walker's original Belle Tout lighthouse on their high point. This is the original position of the lighthouse after its construction in 1828.

Opposite page, bottom: A hundred-year-old card that shows the Belle Tout tower when it was still the only lighthouse at Beachy Head. The curtains in the lantern room have been drawn back enough for us to see 6 circular reflectors, in front of each would have been an Argand lamp. Outside the tower the keeper and his family have been posed by the photographer.

BEACHY HEAD LIGHTHOUSE, EASTBOURNE   26

The New Lighthouse at Beachy Head.

Above: By 1902 the original fog-bound tower on top of Beachy Head cliffs had been replaced by this graceful structure – a pillar rock manned by the three keepers that lived inside it. This sepia card was posted in 1951, suggesting that its coloured band and lantern were still in their original black colour to make them stand out against white cliffs when viewed from seaward. At some point after this they were repainted bright red – the colours they are today. The substantial landing stage attached to the landward side of the tower meant that keeper reliefs could be accomplished by boat so a helideck was never required at Beachy Head.

Left: A very accurate artist's drawing of the 'new' Beachy Head lighthouse from sea level dating from 1907. It's low tide, and lying in front of the tower appears to be some kind of debris left from the construction of the tower. It was possible – but dangerous – to walk from the tower to the foreshore under the cliffs at this state of the tide, and a subsequent walkway built by Trinity House made this a bit easier. Once ashore it was impossible for the keepers to get much further as the cliffs at this point are almost vertical.

Position:	English Channel, 3 mls SW of Eastbourne, East Sussex
Constructed:	2 separate towers, 1828 & 1902
Designers:	James Walker, Thomas Matthews
Builders:	James Walker, Messrs Bullivant & Co.
Present Tower ht:	142ft (43m)
Light character:	W Gp Fl (2) ev 20 secs
Range:	20 mls
Fog warning:	Horn (1) ev 30 secs
Helideck:	None
Automated:	July 1983

BELL ROCK

Bell Rock Lighthouse   Valentines Series

Left: An early sepia view of Bell Rock lighthouse from about 1870 showing the tower at low tide. The flat craggy nature of the Bell or Inchcape Rock is seen clearly, together with the silhouettes of two figures down on the reef.

Right: A much clearer and closer view of the tower at high tide showing how it appears to rise straight out of the North Sea. We can see that a lot more equipment has been attached to the lantern, including an exploding fog signal device and weather vane.

BELL ROCK LIGHTHOUSE, ARBROATH

Bell Rock lighthouse was the first of the great Scottish rock lights to be built by a member of the Stevenson family. From 1807–11 Robert Stevenson and a gang of dedicated workmen toiled on a low lying, serrated sandstone reef south-east of Arbroath to produce the first permanent beacon on what was described as a 'frightful bar to navigation'.

This was indeed a herculean task as the entire reef was covered by every high tide, allowing only a few precious hours either side of low water to excavate the foundations and lay the first courses of masonry. Its construction was dramatic and exciting as the workforce lodged in a wooden barrack raised on legs next to the tower to allow every possible minute of work.

Since its first flash in 1811 there have been several notable incidents in its history, including shelling by enemy aircraft in 1940 and a particularly disastrous fire in 1987 which delayed its conversion to automatic operation by a few months.

Bell Rock has never needed a helideck – there was room for a helipad on the actual reef, although reliefs were only possible at low tide. Today its lantern is draped with a massive net to prevent sea birds roosting on the gallery and fouling the solar panels. The Bell Rock lighthouse remains the oldest British pillar rock lighthouse that continues its nightly warning from the original tower.

Position:	North Sea, 12 mls SE of Arbroath, Tayside
Constructed:	1807–11
Designer:	Robert Stevenson
Builder:	Robert Stevenson
Tower height:	118ft (36m)
Light character:	W Fl ev 5 secs
Range:	18 mls
Fog warning:	Discontinued 1988
Helideck:	None
Automated:	October 1988

SKERRYVORE

Skerryvore Lighthouse, Scotland. (Photo Copyright.)
One of Britain's most famous Lights.
Tower 158 feet high.
Light 12,000 C. Power visible 18 miles.
185,000

Position:	Atlantic Ocean, 12 mls SW of Tiree, Inner Hebrides
Constructed:	1838–44
Designer:	Alan, and later Thomas Stevenson
Builder:	Alan Stevenson
Tower height:	138ft (42m)
Light character:	W Fl ev 10 secs
Range:	23 mls
Fog warning:	Discontinued October 2005
Helideck:	None
Automated:	March 1994

If I had to choose just one British rock light as my favourite then it would undoubtedly be Skerryvore. For no better reason than it was the first rock light I saw – not close up, but from 12 miles away. Even at that distance I could see its slender and graceful silhouette. When I eventually set foot on Skerryvore reef, some years later, its beauty and grandeur were even more magnificent than in all the photographs of it I had seen.

It's one of those structures that has both function and beauty, a difficult balance to achieve, especially when you consider that it was built between 1838–1844 by a 27-year-old engineer who had only built one shore-based lighthouse before coming to Skerryvore.

Again, its stirring history is too lengthy to go into much detail here, but if you are unaware of the dramas of its construction and subsequent history, then you should head for any good book about British lighthouses. Here you will find tales of storm and tempest destroying a wooden-legged barrack and moving an iron anvil 13 yards from where it was left overnight. The workmen were marooned in the replacement barrack by a storm that lasted seven weeks and prevented any supplies reaching them, and as late as 1954 the whole tower was gutted by a disastrous fire that drove the keepers onto the reef itself to await rescue. It was another five years before the lighthouse was fully operational again.

Its builder, Alan Stevenson, was the son of Robert who built Bell Rock. He was a gifted and talented engineer, but sadly only built ten more lighthouses after Skerryvore, none of which was a rock light. He died prematurely in 1865.

There was enough room for a helipad to be built adjacent to the base of the tower in 1972 so Skerryvore has never needed a helideck to spoil its lantern. But even this helipad has suffered tragedy – a rogue wave swamped a relief helicopter before it could lift off in March 1978. There were no casualties, but it was a timely reminder that even in calm conditions Skerryvore reef should never be taken for granted.

Left: A typical Lighthouse Literature Mission postcard from 1910 with some (amended) technical details about Skerryvore. On the reef are two keepers awaiting a relief.

Below: A sectional view of the tower showing the room arrangements and masonry patterns in the various courses.

Skerryvore Lighthouse. Scotland, West Coast.
Internal arrangements of the Tower.—1st Floor, Entrance and Water Tank. 2nd, Coal Store. 3rd, Workshop. 4th, Storeroom. 5th, Kitchen. 6th, Bedroom. 7th, Bedroom. 8th, Library. 9th, Oil Store. 10th, Lightroom. 11th, Lantern.

DUBH ARTACH

Above: Another Lighthouse Literature Mission card showing Dubh Artach on its isolated lump of black basalt. In 1910, when this card was posted, the lighthouse was known as Dhu Heartach – a probable corruption of a Gaelic phrase meaning 'the black one of death'! Dubh Artach was adopted as the anglicised spelling from 1964. The remains of the iron barrack legs are clearly visible, and to their left we can see the derrick used on relief days.

Dubh Artach is another of the great Scottish rock lighthouses built by the Stevenson family between 1867–72, in this case by brothers David and Thomas – the second and third sons of Robert.

It's only 20 miles from Skerryvore and bears a striking resemblance to it, although at 126ft its tower is shorter. It was a particularly difficult lighthouse to build because of its exposed position at the head of a submarine trench that funnelled huge amounts of water directly over this isolated whaleback rock. The working season was short and regularly interrupted by dramatic shows of force from the sea.

Its engineers were well aware of exactly how bad things could get at Dubh Artach. David wrote in his account of building the lighthouse, 'It is believed that at no lighthouse tower hitherto constructed have such remarkable proofs of the violence of the sea at high levels been observed.'

When Dubh Artach was manned its relief could be a very uncomfortable affair for everyone involved. If the sea was calm enough for an open boat to get close, the keepers had to be transferred on the end of a rope from an iron walkway projecting into the considerable surf. Reliefs were frequently overdue by weeks until the remains of the iron legs that supported the barrack used in its construction were removed and a helipad laid instead.

The broad red stripe around its tower was added in 1890 to distinguish it from the nearby Skerryvore in daylight. Automation came comparatively early – in 1971 – as it was still possible for helicopter reliefs to be delayed because of white water rolling over the helipad. Today Dubh Artach has been fitted with banks of solar panels around the lantern to provide its energy.

Interestingly, in 1850 – before Alan Stevenson had set foot on Dubh Artach – he had a son called Robert Louis, who declined to follow his father into lighthouse construction but went on to make his mark in a different field. He once wrote, 'Whenever I smell salt water, I know I am not far from the works of my ancestors.'

Below: A card made from an artist's impression of a vessel called *Amity* passing uncomfortably close by Dubh Artach. He has certainly got the amount of white water breaking over the rock correct, but the tower itself should only have one broad red stripe around its midriff, and not the red and white halves shown in this view.

Position:	Atlantic Ocean, 14 mls SW of Iona, Inner Hebrides
Constructed:	1867–72
Designer:	David & Thomas Stevenson
Builder:	David & Thomas Stevenson, and Alan Brebner
Tower height:	126ft (38m)
Light character:	W Gp Fl (2) ev 30 secs
Range:	20 mls
Fog warning:	Discontinued
Helideck:	None
Automated:	October 1988

SKERVUILE

SKERVUILE LIGHTHOUSE, JURA.

Position:	Sound of Jura, 2½ mls E of Ardfernal, Jura
Constructed:	1865
Designer:	David & Thomas Stevenson
Builder:	David & Thomas Stevenson
Tower height:	83ft (25m)
Light character:	W Fl ev 15 secs
Range:	9 mls
Fog warning:	Discontinued
Automated:	1945

Left: Millpond conditions in the Sound of Jura on what looks like a relief day at Skervuile. We can see a couple of figures on the iron walkway that lead from the landing jetty to the base of the ladder to the door. A sack of something is in the process of being winched into one of the upper rooms.

Below: The background scenery looks stunning, but the main subject is a row of very ordinary cottages where the keepers of Skervuile lighthouse lived when they weren't on duty in the Sound of Jura. Produced in about 1910, it's probably a card that wouldn't attract many sales to visitors, but a lot of lighthouse families used to send this sort of card between the different lighthouses, particularly the remote ones, to keep in touch with their friends and colleagues before the use of the telephone became widespread.

Skervuile (sometimes spelt Skeir Maoile) is gaelic for 'iron rock' – presumably a reference to the obduracy of this tiny flat clump of rock that rises from the Sound of Jura. Small though it may be, it was nevertheless big enough for the steamer *Chevalier* to be lost after striking it in about 1860.

There had been a general clamour for Skervuile to be lit long before this particularly tragedy, but it was at this time the NLB was having difficulties getting the Board of Trade to approve its plans for proposed lights around Scotland. Skervuile was one of the unfortunate sites that remained unlit for 5 years because the Board refused to accept estimates for plans which they had already approved!

However by 1865 David and Thomas Stevenson had built quite a striking pillar light without too much difficulty. The 30ft high solid base is built from granite blocks, while above this the four living rooms have brick walls.

Eighty years later, in 1945, the keepers were withdrawn as a system had been developed to enable the acetylene powered light to be switched on and off automatically using a 'sun' valve.

SKERVUILE SHORE STATION, JURA.

CHICKEN ROCK

CHICKEN ROCK LIGHTHOUSE - PORT ST MARY IOM

The chicken from which this isolated lump of rock off the southern tip of the Isle of Man gets its name is the storm petrel, a sea bird also known as Mother Carey's Chicken that used it as a favourite perch.

Until 1869 they had this rock to themselves, but in this year David and Thomas Stevenson arrived to erect a lighthouse. It was a replacement for two smaller towers erected on the nearby Calf of Man in 1818. Unfortunately, being at some height above sea level they were frequently enveloped with sea fogs and became completely unreliable – just like the two original towers at the Needles and Beachy Head earlier in this chapter.

The construction of the tower was relatively uneventful when compared to Bell Rock, Skerryvore or Dubh Artach. In fact its design bears more than a passing resemblance to the latter. No surprise really as its two engineers were working on both towers at the same time.

Chicken Rock hit the national headlines in December 1960 when a disastrous fire swept through the tower and forced the keepers to abandon it by sliding down ropes from the lantern gallery onto the reef itself. Only a brave and heroic rescue by the Port St Mary and Port Erin lifeboats saved the stranded keepers' lives. The NLB decided that at the same time as repairing the tower it would be automated. This was completed in September 1962 – comparatively early for a rock light in British lighthouse history.

Position:	Irish Sea, 3mls S of Isle of Man
Constructed:	1869–74
Designer:	David & Thomas Stevenson
Builder:	David & Thomas Stevenson, and Alan Brebner
Tower height:	144ft (44m)
Light character:	W Fl ev 5 secs
Range:	21 mls
Fog warning:	Discontinued June 2005
Helideck:	None
Automated:	September 1962

749   CHICKENS ROCK LIGHTHOUSE, I.o.M.

Far left: Compare this view of Chicken Rock with the earlier one of Dubh Artach and the similarities are striking. When Dubh Artach was only half complete, David and Thomas Stevenson started work on an almost identical tower on Chicken Rock.

Left: This sepia view of Chicken Rock from the south shows its proximity to the island known as the Calf of Man. To the left of the tower we can see the outline of one of the two 1818 towers that this lighthouse replaced. Also, down on the reef itself are three keepers – confirming that it was taken prior to the disastrous 1960 fire.

THE SMALLS

The Smalls Light-house.

Left: Proof, if such were needed, that there was no subject too remote or too obscure for early postcard publishers! One wonders where a card showing an open boat being rowed from a relief vessel with the new keepers and fresh supplies as part of the relief of the Smalls lighthouse – 21 miles from the nearest mainland – would have been sold, and who would have bought it? Lighthouse keepers and their families perhaps – as a record of their place of work – but today a card such as this is highly sought after as its rarity and unusual subject make it very attractive to card collectors.

Position:	St George's Channel, 21 mls W of St Ann's Head, Pembrokeshire
Constructed:	1775–76 &1859–61
Designers:	Henry Whiteside, James Walker
Builders:	Henry Whiteside, James & Nicholas Douglass
Present Tower ht:	133ft (41m)
Light character:	W Gp Fl (3) ev 15 secs & Fxd Red
Range:	W 25 mls, R 13 mls
Fog warning:	Horn (2) ev 60 secs
Helideck:	1987
Automated:	September 1987

The Smalls lighthouse is one of Britain's most famous lighthouses, yet its remoteness means it's rarely seen at first hand. It's the most isolated lighthouse maintained by Trinity House – rising from the last of a series of islands and reefs that stretch seaward for 20 miles from the Pembrokeshire coast.

The present granite tower is the second Smalls lighthouse – its predecessor was a unique wooden stilted beacon erected by Henry Whiteside in 1776. The story of its construction and subsequent history encompasses every conceivable problem in building and manning an isolated lighthouse; poor weather, marooned workmen, overdue reliefs, the death of a keeper, a change in lighthouse keeping policy, culminating in an increasingly unstable structure that led to its eventual replacement in stone. For

a story of derring-do, determination, and bravery read a full account of the Smalls lighthouses.

Whiteside's unique lighthouse consisted of an octagonal wooden structure with a lantern on top raised over 70ft in the air by a circle of oak legs. It only took just over a year to build, but within months was suffering much torment from winter storms and had to be strengthened. During this time Whiteside and the keepers were marooned on the Smalls; things got so bad and food ran short that they had to resort to sending messages in bottles!

Sometime around 1800, one of the two keepers died. His companion, unwilling to dispose of the body in case he was accused of murder, fashioned a crude coffin for the corpse and tied it to the lantern gallery where it remained for several weeks – the weather being too severe to effect a relief. When

rescued, the remaining keeper was in a state of complete exhaustion and near hysteria. Ever since this incident three keepers were assigned to every British lighthouse, to ensure the remaining two could continue their duties if one died.

The wooden beacon continued to deteriorate until it was obvious it would have to be replaced before the sea swept it away. James Walker designed a graceful stepped-base 133ft granite tower built by James and Nicholas Douglass between 1859–61. It was the first rock light to have a toilet in one of its lower rooms and an early wind generator attached to the lantern roof. Red and white bands were added to make the tower a prominent seamark sometime after it was built, and in 1997 they were removed after its automation ten years previously.

2 ISLAND LIGHTS

Muckle Flugga Lighthouse, Unst, Shetland.

Above: There are few more isolated and wild parts of the United Kingdom than this bleak cluster of islands known collectively as the Burrafirth Holms. They were given names such as Vesta Skerry, Cliff Skerry and Rumblings, but the highest of the group was Muckle Flugga and on it David and Thomas Stevenson built a modest tower with a mighty location. It was, until its automation, the most northerly inhabited building in the United Kingdom and its remoteness places it nearer to the capital of Norway than to the capital of Scotland.

Although still classed as rock stations, our island lighthouses can be equally remote as the more spectacular pillar lights. The remotest British lighthouse of all – Sule Skerry – is an island lighthouse, 40 miles west of Orkney. The difference is, of course, that their engineers had the luxury of enough room to build keepers' accommodation either adjacent to, or attached to the tower itself.

Some island lights have comparatively spacious and stylish accommodation despite the remoteness of their position. Most island lights also had room for the keepers to stretch their legs outside the lighthouse; to fish, keep animals, grow their own food or even play golf!

Sadly though, all island lighthouses are now automatic like the pillar lights. For some islands the only human presence on them has now gone leaving the weeds to grow where there was once a neatly-kept vegetable garden.

ROUND ISLAND

Above: This aerial view of Round Island gives us a good idea of the difficulties of landing materials for its construction. The only place that was sheltered enough for this operation was in the gulley on the right-hand side of the card – protected by Camber Rocks. The pathway from the landing stage to the lighthouse is clearly visible in this 1962 card.

Right: This is the view of Round Island from the uninhabited island of St Helen's. The small code number 11017 on the left-hand side of the card indicates that the photograph was taken prior to 1895 which means the lighthouse was, at most, eight years old. It was posted in March 1905, and its sender – someone called Bunnie – remarks that, '. . . the wind is beginning to howl again now', not an unusual event in the Scilly Isles.

Position:	English Channel, northernmost Scilly island
Constructed:	1886–87
Designer:	James Douglass
Builder:	William Douglass
Tower height:	63ft (19m)
Light character:	W Fl ev 10 secs
Range:	24 mls
Fog warning:	Horn (4) ev 60 secs
Automated:	1988

Round Island is the most northerly of the Scillies group, an uninhabited lump of granite 130ft high that drops sheer on all sides into the Atlantic below. Its summit is relatively flat and spacious, and given its strategic position at the entrance to the English Channel, it became an obvious candidate for a lighthouse.

In 1886 Trinity House and William Douglass arrived to build a lighthouse designed by his father, James Douglass. It had a circular granite tower 63ft high with a keeper's cottage and foghorn attached. Building the tower wasn't particularly difficult, but landing the men and materials was. There was no obvious landing place so one had to be built at the southern end of the island in the lee of a small islet.

To help land the building materials huge blocks of stone were cemented around and in between the natural contours of the rock to form a flat landing platform and flights of steps to and from it. There was even an aerial ropeway used for delivering heavy and bulky items to the top of the island. This landing was subsequently used for reliefs, and by the day trippers the lighthouse used to attract, until helicopters came along and could set down almost next to the door of the lighthouse.

When the light first became operational in 1887 it was unusual in that it showed a red flash. Red light doesn't travel as far as white light so to increase its range it was fitted with one of the largest hyper-radial optics ever seen in a British lighthouse – only two others of a similar size ever existed. This gave unbroken service until 1967 when modernisation saw it replaced by something equally quirky – a bank of revolving car headlight bulbs – or sealed-beam units as they are officially known. These too were removed when automation came in 1988 and the keepers left.

Round Island, Scilly Isles   Valentine's Series

nice & calm bt the wind is beginning to howl agn now. Love Bunnie

CASQUETS

The Channel Islands have long been known as 'the graveyard of the Channel' because of the number and ferocity of the isolated rocks and jagged ledges that rear from the waters around them. Alderney is the nearest to the French coast, and eight miles off its west coast rise a particularly menacing line of sandstone rocks, about 600ft long, 100ft high called the Casquets.

Thomas le Cocq, who actually owned the Casquets, was pressurised by local ship owners that had lost vessels on his rocks, and he in turn asked Trinity House for a patent to erect a lighthouse – which he got in June 1723. By October of the following year three towers, called St Peter, St Thomas and Dungeon, were visible on the Casquets. Each contained a coal fire in a glazed lantern, an attempt to give the Casquets a unique character to any other light on the English or French coast.

By 1790 the inefficient coal fires had gone, replaced by Argand lamps in front of polished reflectors, and even these were replaced in 1818 by revolving apparatus. But the efficiency of the station was never highly regarded, mainly because the three lights were unsynchronised and seafarers rarely saw three distinct flashes. An increase in height by 30ft for all three towers in 1854 did little to improve matters, so in 1877 two of the towers were discontinued. The remaining tower, St Peter, resplendent in its red and white hoops, contains the lantern today, while St Thomas has a helideck on top of it, and the other – Dungeon – was converted to house the foghorn.

Far left: Looking more like a fortress on a rocky outcrop, this is the Casquets lighthouse complex. On the far left is the main tower, St Peter, that now houses the lantern. To its right is St Thomas that has now been converted into a helipad, while over to the right topped by a black foghorn is Dungeon.

Below: Another view of the Casquets in a hand-drawn card where the jaggedness of the reef is matched by the wildness of the waves. A sailing vessel is passing uncomfortably close by the three towers that once supported coal-burning grates in glazed lanterns until 1877.

THE CASQUETS LIGHTHOUSE OFF ALDERNEY.

Position:	English Channel, 5 mls W of Alderney, Channel islands
Constructed:	1723–24 & 1854
Designer:	Thomas le Cocq,
Builder:	Thomas le Cocq & William Norman
Tower height:	45ft (14m), & 75ft (23m)
Light character:	Fixed white, W Gp Fl (5) ev 30 secs
Range:	Unknown & 24 mls
Fog warning:	Horn (2) ev 60 secs
Automated:	December 1990

The Casquets Light House 1874.

COQUET

COQUET ISLAND. 85948 K.K/C

Coquet island was recognised as a problem for coastal navigation back in the 1830s. It's a low-lying jumble of sand dunes and sandstone a mile from the Northumberland coast near Amble. The sandstone was quarried for the tower, while the dunes attract thousands of nesting sea birds – terns and puffins in particular – to the RSPB reserve on the island during the summer.

Coquet is an interesting lighthouse because of its architecture. It has a square tower – not unique for Trinity House, but quite rare. Around the top of the 72ft tower is a magnificent castellated parapet, the walls of which are 3ft thick, giving it the appearance of being fortified. The sturdy keepers' accommodation was in fact built on the remains of a Benedictine monastery at the south-west corner of the island. James Walker was the architect and it was completed by 1841 at a cost of £3,268.

For over 130 years paraffin vapour lamps provided the light. Electricity didn't arrive until 1976, while just 14 years later, in 1990, the keepers departed as automation took over. Its warning white and red flash is now produced from 12 sealed-beam units, the white visible for 21 miles and the red for 16. Since a modernisation programme in April 2007 they have been powered by a bank of 68 solar panels.

There is some interesting folklore connected with Coquet that claims one of the first keepers to man the lighthouse was William Darling, the elder brother of Grace Darling. Not only that, it was while visiting Coquet island that she is supposed to have caught the chill that turned into tuberculosis and led to her untimely demise in October 1842 at the age of 26 – just four years after her heroic deeds at the Longstone lighthouse.

Position:	North Sea, 4 mls SE of Alnmouth, Northumberland
Constructed:	1840–41
Designer:	James Walker
Builder:	James Walker
Tower height:	72ft (22m)
Light character:	W+R Gp Fl (3) ev 30 secs
Range:	W21, R16 mls
Fog warning:	Horn (1) ev 30 secs
Automated:	December 1990

Above: It's 1914, World War I is underway and Coquet lighthouse is over 60 years old. The square tower is one of only two in the Trinity House Service and the decorative parapet of the lantern gallery is seen to good effect. The substantial keepers' house behind it is part of a former Benedictine monastery. The whole complex is now a Grade II Listed Building.

On the rocky foreshore we can see three figures – probably the lighthouse keepers posing for the photograph. Today, a photograph from the same spot would show a much brighter scene. The top half of the lighthouse tower and the keepers house have all been painted white.

INNER FARNE

The Farnes are a cluster of about 25 low-lying and rocky islands situated about 7 miles off the Northumberland coast. There are two distinct clusters; the Inner and Outer Farnes, which are separated by Staples Sound. Both groups have seen their fair share of maritime casualties. Lighting these dangerous reefs was accomplished in a rather haphazard manner with the construction, modification, abandonment or demolition of several towers, of varying effectiveness, placed on several of the islands in the group.

The light on the Inner Farne was part of this process. The original tower of 1778 had a coal-fired beacon on top but its efficiency was poorly regarded and Trinity House replaced it in 1811 with the present lighthouse, a small 43ft high tower designed by Daniel Alexander with Argand lamps and reflectors. Its outward appearance – with gallery railings that lean outwards and a number of stout exterior metal stays joining the lantern gallery to the lantern roof – is extremely similar to Samuel Wyatt's original tower on the Longships that suffered much torment from the sea before being replaced.

In 1910 the Inner Farne light was the earliest Trinity House light to be converted to automatic operation, over 60 years before the clamour for automation began in earnest. An acetylene light controlled by a 'sun valve' was installed. This mechanism, an invention of the Swedish lighthouse engineer Gustaf Dalen, consists of an arrangement of reflective gold-plated copper bars supporting a suspended black rod; when lit by the sun the black rod absorbs the direct heat and that reflected from the other bars and expands downwards, thereby cutting off the supply of acetylene gas. The reverse would happen at sunrise.

It required no day-to-day maintenance so the keepers could be withdrawn. This system remained in operation until the lighthouse was further modernised and converted to solar-powered operation in late 1996. The National Trust bought the island of Inner Farne for £132,000 in 2005 which included the keepers' cottage and the acetylene house although the lighthouse tower is still maintained and owned by Trinity House.

FI.1.   THE LIGHTHOUSE. FARNE ISLAND.   Copyright APS.

Left: There's very little else on Inner Farne apart from the lighthouse and a couple of ruins. This is the lighthouse, but more prominent in this view is the stark architecture of the 'acetylene house' with the three round windows. This stored the acetylene gas that enabled Inner Farne to be Trinity House's earliest automatic light in 1910.

Below: A colourful hand-painted card from 1906 with flags flying at Inner Farne light. One of the keepers poses in the foreground and a further eight people are lined up in front of the keepers' cottages.

Position:	North Sea, 3 mls N of Seahouses
Constructed:	1778, 1811
Designer:	J Blackett, Daniel Alexander
Builder:	J Blackett, Daniel Alexander
Tower height:	43ft (13m)
Light character:	W+R Gp Fl (2) ev 15 secs
Range:	W 10, R 7 mls
Fog warning:	None
Automated:	1910

INNER FARNE LIGHTHOUSE

LONGSTONE

The second of the Farne Islands lighthouses is the famous Longstone lighthouse, although strictly speaking it should perhaps be known as Outer Farne as it sits on Longstone rock, the outermost reef of the group. It was built between 1825–26 by Joseph Nelson as part of an attempt to rationalise and improve the navigation around the islands. Inside its rather sturdy boundary wall was an 85ft tower with a keepers' house attached.

Its lighting on 15th February saw the closure of the nearby Brownsman Island light, so the keeper was transferred to Longstone. He was called William Darling and with him came his wife and 11 year-old daughter Grace. Twelve years later she was to become more famous than anyone could have imagined. Her heroic deeds in September 1838 when she helped her father rescue the survivors from the wreck of the *Forfarshire* brought her, and the Longstone lighthouse, well and truly into the limelight.

She only lived four more years, but there's still a plaque in the room that used to be Grace's bedroom commemorating the event, even though there are no longer any keepers to look at it. They left in September 1990 when the station was automated. Longstone still has crowds of visitors in the summer months that come to watch the birds and the seals, and to photograph the rather striking red and white tower of the lighthouse – the home of a heroine.

Above: The low, rocky nature of the Longstone reef is apparent in this sepia card. Projecting from the roof of the keepers' accommodation are two large foghorns. The curious domed structure on the right is something of a mystery. It's probably a store for goods that have to be kept dry such as coal. In later years its dome was removed and a wireless antenna erected in it, but this has subsequently been removed leaving just a circular wall.

Left: This is an earlier view of the same light from a different angle. The foghorn isn't quite as impressive, but we can see how the wall of the courtyard that surrounds the keepers' accommodation is slightly curved at the base to lessen the effects of the heavy seas on it. The biggest difference is in the design of the lantern roof. This view shows the original roof before it was changed for a Trinity House 'ventilated' lantern roof.

Longstone Lighthouse, Farne Islands

Auty Series. G.H. N/C. 475

Position:	North Sea, 18 mls SE of Berwick, Northumberland
Constructed:	1825–26
Designer:	Joseph Nelson
Builder:	Joseph Nelson
Tower height:	85ft (26m)
Light character:	W Fl ev 20 secs
Range:	24 mls
Fog warning:	Horn (2) ev 60 secs
Automated:	September 1990

BASS ROCK

Our tour around the coast of Britain now brings us into Scotland where successive generations of the Stevenson family built some of the finest lighthouses we have. Bass Rock is a 350ft high plug of volcanic lava in the Firth of Forth, 3 miles from North Berwick. It has had a long and interesting history – the addition of a lighthouse is comparatively recent. St Baldred lived on the Rock in the 7th century and a chapel, now ruined, was built on the site of his cell. It was actually owned by the Lauder family from 1316, and then sold to the government in 1671, who rebuilt an older fortress as a prison. Between 1672 and 1688 some 40 political and religious prisoners are said to have died in the dungeons on the rock.

The lighthouse was built on the only flat area large enough to house it – the site of the gun emplacements from the former fortress – which meant that it actually faces towards the Scottish coast. David Alan Stevenson built a 66ft tower on this ledge between 1901–02 and it was lit for the first time on 1st November 1902.

There are no keepers left of course, they were withdrawn when it was automated in December 1988, but there are thousands of other inhabitants – seabirds! Almost every available inch is occupied by razorbills, guillemots, cormorants, puffins, eider ducks and various gull species, but outnumbering all of these is the gannet with a breeding colony of 30–40,000 pairs, making Bass Rock a mecca for international ornithologists. The fight for nesting space in the summer can be intense and ferocious, and its summit can turn white with their guano. It is the largest single-rock gannetry in the world. Indeed, the North Atlantic Gannet's Latin name is *Morus bassana* after the rock.

Position:	Firth of Forth, 3 mls NE of North Berwick, Lothian
Constructed:	1902
Designer:	David A. Stevenson
Builder:	David A. Stevenson
Tower height:	66ft (20m)
Light character:	W Gp Fl (3) ev 20 secs
Range:	10 mls
Fog warning:	Discontinued
Automated:	December 1988

Far left: An impressive painting of Bass Rock lighthouse showing how it was built on top of a ruined fortress on what must have been the only level piece of ground on the whole rock.

Left: A closer view of David Alan Stevenson's lighthouse with the prison ruins in the foreground. The steps to the left lead to the summit of the island and the largest single-rock gannetry in the world.

FIDRA & INCHKEITH

Vessels heading into the Firth of Forth towards the port of Leith had to be especially watchful for a couple of islands that needed careful navigation. Because of their position in such an important inlet, and being so close to the Northern Lighthouse Board headquarters in George Street, Edinburgh, they soon became candidates for a lighthouse.

Inchkeith was the first; it received a most imposing light and keepers' accommodation in the grounds of an earlier 16th century fort in September 1804. This is now listed as being of historical and architectural importance. The island has had a colourful past – it has been at various times a seat of Pictish Kings, a base for early Christian Evangelists, an isolation colony for the plague victims, a medieval fortress, a victim of siege and blockade, the scene of a gory battle, and a site for heavy guns during two world wars. Most of these have gradually been overtaken by dereliction and the encroaching undergrowth – apart from Thomas Smith's 62ft tower (which was actually built by Robert Stevenson) on the summit of the island. The tower (now painted an interesting shade of brown)

is built on top of a parapetted accommodation block with a spacious courtyard in front. This was where the helicopters landed to change the keepers – an unnecessary operation since July 1986 when it was automated.

Fidra is a rocky island little more than half a mile off the Lothian coast and only 5½ miles west of Bass Rock. Thomas and David A. Stevenson built a lighthouse and keepers houses on its summit without undue concern and lit it for the first time in 1885. Their biggest problem involved the compulsory purchase of the land from its owners – the Dirleton Estate – who immediately claimed compensation for the damage caused by the noise of a foghorn on the island, even though the Northern Lighthouse Board had no plans to install one! Harsh words were apparently said by Lord Young, who heard the case, about anyone who thought a fog signal 'more disagreeable than a quiet shipwreck.' Fidra was the first of the NLB's lights to go completely automatic and be monitored by remote control in October 1970 after a submarine cable brought electricity to the island.

FIDRA	
Position:	Firth of Forth, 15 mls NE of Leith, Lothian
Constructed:	1885
Designer:	Thomas & David A.Stevenson
Builder:	Thomas & David A.Stevenson
Tower height:	56ft (17m)
Light character:	W Gp Fl (4) ev 30 secs
Range:	20 mls
Fog warning:	None
Automated:	October 1970

INCHKEITH	
Position:	Firth of Forth, 5 mls N of Leith, Lothian
Constructed:	1803–04
Designer:	Thomas Smith
Builder:	Robert Stevenson
Tower height:	62ft (19m)
Light character:	W Fl ev 15 secs
Range:	22 mls
Fog warning:	Discontinued
Automated:	July 1986

Inchkeith, Firth of Forth

ISLAND OF FIDRA AND LIGHTHOUSE.

Far left: Inchkeith blocks a direct approach to the Forth Bridge by shipping which has to pass north or south of it. Its lighthouse sits on the summit of an island littered with the remnants of a colourful and varied past.

Left: Fidra Island is much smaller and has an interesting natural arch through it. This sepia card shows the light and the keepers' houses before the bricks were painted white.

ISLE OF MAY

Straddling the mouth of the Firth of Forth, 5 miles from the Fife coast, is the rocky Isle of May, a popular location for assorted monastic dwellings and retreats during medieval times. It also has a large breeding population of seabirds – guillemots, gulls, shags, kittiwakes, razorbills and puffins in particular – so it was a natural choice for the British Trust of Ornithology to set up a Bird Observatory there in 1934. In 1956 it was declared a National Nature Reserve.

However, the real significance of the Isle of May is that it was the site chosen for Scotland's very first lighthouse. In 1635, long before the NLB came into being, Charles I granted a patent to James Maxwell of Innerwick and John and Alexander Cunningham of Barnes to erect a beacon on the Isle of May and to collect dues from shipping for its maintenance. It was a crude affair consisting of a 40ft stone tower with a coal burning iron grate on its roof. The 400 tons of coal it consumed each year coal were hauled up the tower in sacks with a pulley by the three men employed to attend to the fire. In 1790 fumes from this grate suffocated a lightkeeper's entire family.

Besides killing its attendants, it wasn't a very efficient lighthouse because the character of the light was affected by wind, smoke and weather which made it particularly unreliable. It could also be mistaken for the flames belching from lime kilns on the Fife coast. On 19th December 1810, HMS *Nymphe* and *Pallas* were wrecked near Dunbar when they mistook the flames from a lime kiln for the navigation light on the Isle of May. Because of this, in 1814 the Commissioners of Northern Lighthouses (who had been established since 1786) purchased the Isle of May from the Duke of Portland, together with the right to collect annual light dues of £60,000.

Robert Stevenson was engaged to effect improvements and constructed an elaborate 78ft square stone tower with castellated parapets

Position:	Firth of Forth, 12 mls N of Dunbar, Lothian
Constructed:	1636, 1816
Designer:	James Maxwell and J&A Cunningham, Robert Stevenson
Builder:	James Maxwell and J&A Cunningham, Robert Stevenson
Tower height:	40ft (12m), 78ft (24m)
Light character:	W Gp Fl (2) ev 15 secs
Range:	22 mls
Fog warning:	Discontinued
Automated:	March 1989

Above: A magnificent sepia card from 1914 that gives us the opportunity to compare the first lighthouse on the Isle of May and the present one. The square white structure on the left is the remains of the 1636 stone tower with a coal-burning grate on its roof. It's dwarfed by the Gothic splendour of Robert Stevenson's 1816 masterpiece that had spacious accommodation for visiting NLB officials but not enough for all the lightkeepers! In the foreground three young ladies in their summer hats sit on the grass and watch the photographer at work.

in a Gothic style rising from an equally grand accommodation block. It was lit on 1st February 1816. A smaller 'low light' tower was added on the east side of the island in April 1844 to act, in conjunction with the main light, as an indicator of the treacherous North Carr rock some 7 miles to the north. When the North Carr lightship was established on station in 1887, the low light became redundant and it was discontinued although the buildings remain.

Further improvements saw the first British fixed dioptric light installed in September 1836, but in June 1885 work began on an elaborate upgrade. The ornate 1816 tower had plenty of rooms for visiting officials, but accommodation for only three lightkeepers and their families. Dwellings were needed for three more, together with an engine house, boiler house, workshop and coal store for the generation of electricity. These were built in a small valley on the island containing a freshwater loch, 270 yards from the light and 175 feet below it. Two generators, each weighing about 4½ tons – the largest so far made – had a capacity of 8,800 watts, which could be controlled so that the whole or only part of the current was used.

From 1st December 1886 the new light gave four flashes in quick succession every 30 seconds. When only one generator was used about three million candlepower could be produced, but double that when both were used – about 300 or 600 times more powerful than the old fixed oil light. Its range was officially 22 miles, but sometimes the 'loom' of the light could be seen at 40 and 50 miles distant when it reflected off clouds overhead.

It became a rock station on 9th August 1972 when the families left for houses in Edinburgh, and the keepers were delivered to the island by helicopter. Their final shift ended on 31st March 1989 when the station was automated.

Below left: An attractive hand-tinted card showing the 1844 Lower light on the east coat of the island that was an early attempt to mark the position of the North Carr rock before the NLB's only lightship was established there in 1887. A lone keeper poses on the gallery.

Below right: Another comparison of the old and new on the Isle of May, this time drawn by an artist in about 1910. The square castellated building is the same one as in the first card, and the circular insert in the bottom right corner shows the coal-burning grate of 1636. The artist has drawn the present tower as though it has been whitewashed, but this is obviously not the case.

MAY ISLAND LOWER LIGHT

PENTLAND SKERRIES

Pentland Skerries, South Ronaldshay.

Left: A very formal portrait taken around 1910 of no fewer than eight lighthouse keepers – four at ground level and four on the top of the abandoned second tower of Thomas Smith's 1794 lighthouse. Although it looks like it has been built from bricks, they are actually blocks of stone.

Most interesting of all is the well-camouflaged donkey standing in front of the second tower. This is the beast that would happily stand for photographs but was nowhere to be seen when there was work to be done unloading the supply ship!

The passage between mainland Scotland and the Orkney islands – known as the Pentland Firth – was a fearful stretch of water before it was lit and not much better in daylight conditions that were usually less than perfect. Ferocious currents, half-hidden rocks and reefs made the longer passage between Orkney and Shetland the preferred route for ships heading for the Atlantic. Some of the most feared obstacles were a group of four uninhabited islands that surfaced in the middle of the eastern approaches to the Firth – an area known as 'Hell's Mouth'. Collectively known as the Pentland Skerries, the largest is Muckle Skerry and on it was built the Pentland Skerries lighthouse.

The Commissioners of Northern Lighthouses had only existed for eight years but were already trying to reduce the dangers of a passage through the Pentland Firth. One of the sites earmarked for some kind of navigation aid was the Pentland Skerries. Although a comparatively early Scottish lighthouse, its construction in 1794 to the designs of Thomas Smith was supervised by a 22 year-old man whose surname and whose family were subsequently to become synonymous with the superb civil engineering of Scottish lighthouses. His name was Robert Stevenson and this was his very first Scottish lighthouse. Within a mere 17 years he was at work on his greatest achievement – the Bell Rock lighthouse, but it all started here.

Stevenson brought a gang of Orkney masons to the Pentland Skerries to build not one but two stone towers, 79ft and 59ft high and 60ft apart. They showed fixed white lights with the help of 66 reflectors in each lantern. Between 1820 and 1833 they were rebuilt on the same site, this time 100ft apart and raised to 118ft and 88ft respectively. In 1847 the reflectors were replaced by refracting glass lenses.

It's reported that the two fixed lights were often

confused for the mast-head lights of a ship – with disastrous consequences. By the late 19th century fixed lights were also no longer regarded as suitable for important landfall lights, so they were replaced in 1895 by a powerful single flashing light. The lower tower was retained to house the fog horn, which projected from the top. It was eventually discontinued in June 2005, eleven years after the automation of the light and removal of the keepers in March 1994.

This lighthouse is notable for the number of its keepers that have received commendations for brave and heroic acts. In June 1871 assistant keeper Donald Montgomery dived into wild seas with a rope to rescue a boy washed overboard from the lifeboat to a Wick fishing boat *Good Desire* that had run aground on the island. All the keepers at the lighthouse were commended in July 1884 for their bravery in rescuing twelve men from the *Vicksberg*, a barque carrying coal from Leith to Canada that was wrecked on the west side. Seven others drowned and their lonely grave, with an inscribed headstone, is found a short distance from the tower. Finally, thick fog in 1965 drove the vessel *Kathe Niederkirchner* ashore on the Skerries. Two assistant keepers climbed down the cliffs to board the ship's lifeboat adrift in the dangerous currents. They brought 50 crew and passengers safely ashore at the east landing.

Compare these heroic deeds with the story of the island's donkey – a somewhat wilful beast employed to carry stores from landing to tower. Blessed with some kind of sixth sense, it seemed to know instinctively when the supply boat was due and there was work to be done. On such occasions it would make for the remotest, most inaccessible part of the island and hide. However, the animal seemed more than happy to pose for photographers!

Below: Here he is again, happily carrying a keeper's wife, mother or daughter (it's difficult to tell!) for another specially posed early 1900s photograph at Ship 'Goe' – which is probably a mispelling of 'Geo'. A geo (from the Old Norse *gjá*) is an inlet, a gully or a narrow and deep cleft in the face of a cliff, particularly in Shetland, Orkney or the Hebrides. The three keepers are wearing their NLB uniforms for this group, and one of the five women is carrying a young baby wrapped in a shawl.

Position:	Pentland Firth, 5 mls NE of Duncansby Head, Highland
Constructed:	1794, 1833
Designer:	Thomas Smith, Robert Stevenson
Builder:	Robert Stevenson
Tower height:	79ft (24m) & 59ft (18m), then 118ft (36m) & 88ft (27m)
Light character:	W Gp Fl (3) ev 30 secs
Range:	25 mls
Fog warning:	Discontinued June 2005
Automated:	March 1994

Ship Goe, Pentland Skerries

STROMA

Position:	Pentland Firth, 5 mls NW of Duncansby Head, Highland
Constructed:	1890, 1896
Designer:	Unknown, D.A. & Charles Stevenson
Builder:	Unknown, D.A. & Charles Stevenson
Tower height:	Unknown, 76ft (23m)
Light character:	W Gp Fl (2) ev 20 secs
Range:	26 mls
Fog warning:	Discontinued June 2005
Automated:	March 1997

Above: Stroma lighthouse looks as though it's just been repainted in this card. The stonework around the windows, doors and under the lantern gallery looks very crisp and new. There's a small cluster of people posing in front of the first cottage to the right of the tower, two of whom look like children, but any further details are impossible to see. This was probably taken while the island had some remaining inhabitants.

Just seven miles west of the Pentland Skerries lies the much larger island of Stroma, once home to a thriving population of crofters, but now, sadly deserted. In 1901, 375 people lived on Stroma, by 1951 this had shrunk to 111, and in 1962 the last family left leaving a resident population of just three – the lighthouse keepers. Over 50 dwellings and two churches still remain on Stroma, but their inhabitants and congregations left for a life on the mainland with its higher wages and a more comfortable way of life. The construction in the 1950s of a nuclear power station at Dounreay, a little over 20 miles away on the Caithness coast finally emptied the island of its permanent population.

Archaeological evidence suggests that early settlers of Stroma were Norsemen who named the island 'Straumsey' – 'the island in the stream'. The 'streams' of course were the fearsome tides that rip through the Pentland Firth. Flood tides from the Atlantic to the North Sea tear past Stroma at anything up to ten knots. West of the island they divide and pass north and south around it, but should there be an easterly wind to produce a swell at the same time as a flood tide then an area of broken water known as The Boars of Duncansby appears. The UK Admiralty guide to the area describes this tidal race as 'extremely violent and dangerous when a SE-going stream is opposed by E and SE gales'.

If that wasn't frightening enough, this is what it says about another tide race close to Stroma. 'The most extensive and dangerous race in the Pentland Firth is called the Merry Men of Mey, which forms off St John's Point during the W-going tidal stream, and when fully established, extends the entire distance across the firth to Tor Ness. The most violent part of the Merry Men of Mey lies over a large sandwave field that lies approximately 3½ miles W of Stroma. In a W sea or swell the entire race becomes very violent; large waves will form very suddenly and come from varying directions, making it difficult to counter or anticipate. Small vessels are advised to remember that the W-going tidal stream emerging from the Outer Sound can be very strong, rates in excess of 10 kts can be expected and the danger of being swept into the race is very real.'

However, most frightening of all, and the main reason why the lighthouse on Stroma was built is because of 'the Swilkie' a violent whirlpool off the northern tip of the island. Caused by the collision of four or five powerful tidal races, the Swilkie swirls and roars at all states of the tide. Again, the Admiralty guide warns, 'The Swilkie persists almost continuously off Swilkie Point where the strong E and W-going main streams through the Outer Sound meet the N-going eddies, which

flow on the E and W sides of Stroma. The Swilkie can be dangerous and should be avoided even in fine weather. It is most violent when the W-going stream through the Outer Sound is opposed by a W gale.'

There is very little known about the first lighthouse built on Swilkie Point apart from the fact that it was constructed between 1889–90 by person or persons unknown, but certainly not the Northern Lighthouse Board. It was believed to have been what is attractively described as a 'scintillating' Trotter-Lindberg type light with a petroleum spirit (lythene) burner that exhibited one white flash every 60 seconds. It probably wasn't terribly efficient because within six years it was being replaced by a modest circular stone tower 79ft high designed by David A. and Charles Stevenson whose light was first seen on 15th October 1896. The lantern contained another

Trotter-Lindberg light – the petroleum spirit was contained in cisterns placed outside the lantern. The light from this was soon inadequate for such a strategic light so a paraffin lamp was substituted for the original, enabling the small tower that carried the lantern also to serve as an oil store instead of requiring a separate building. This in turn was replaced in 1972 by a sealed-beam unit, like the ones at Coquet and Round Island, activated by the flick of a switch. These lasted until 1994 when automation started and they were removed and replaced by the huge 4th order glass lenses and prisms from the recently-automated Sule Skerry light, revolving around a 250W metal halide bulb. In March 1997 everything was finally complete and the keepers withdrawn. Stroma now has no permanent residents, although still attracts many visitors – who land when tides and wind allow!

Left: This is Stroma lighthouse from the sea from where we can see its substantial fog horn tower. The boat from which this was taken would have been fairly close to Stroma's notorious Swilkie whirlpool off the northern tip of the island. I've scanned this card to show its interesting edge detail. This wavy irregular finish to the card is known as a deckled edge and was once popular for a short time, but has now fallen out of favour with postcard publishers.

AUSKERRY

The many islands of Orkney are comparatively well served with lighthouses, and few were problematic in their construction. Such is the case at Auskerry, a small (210 acres) low-lying, flat sandstone island three miles south of Stronsay. David and Thomas Stevenson built the lighthouse, on the southern tip of the island, between 1865–6. The tower is fairly tall (112ft) to give it a range of 18 miles. Originally built from brick, it has subsequently been painted white. It became a rock station in the 1920s which meant the keepers' families lived away from Auskerry. Automation came early – the last keepers were withdrawn in 1961 and the island became uninhabited. In recent times their cottages have been renovated for use as holiday homes.

There's an interesting reminder at Auskerrry that lighthouses were very much regarded as targets during World War II. In the paddock next to the keepers' cottages are two concrete plinths with four bolts protruding. Engraved in the concrete is an inscription 'Hotchkiss Gun 1943'. Close to the second one is a crater from one of two bombs said to have been aimed at the lighthouse, which led to the subsequent installation of the guns. The lighthouse at Pentland Skerries was machine-gunned by an enemy aircraft in February 1941 – which then flew on to do the same at Stroma. No significant damage or loss of life was caused at these lights, unlike the unfortunate events at Fair Isle in December 1941 and Out Skerries a month later.

Position:	North Sea, 14 mls NE of Kirkwall, Orkney
Constructed:	1865–66
Designer:	David & Thomas Stevenson
Builder:	David & Thomas Stevenson
Tower height:	112ft (34m)
Light character:	W Fl ev 20 secs
Range:	18 mls
Fog warning:	None
Automated:	1961

Below: A view from about 1910 showing the brick tower of Auskerry lighthouse and the rather functional architecture of the keepers' accommodation that so many NLB lighthouses seem to possess. Because this view is taken prior to 1920 when it became a rock station, the small group of figures in front of the wall is probably a keeper and his family.

AUSKERRY LIGHHOUSE, STRONSAY   "LEONARD'S ORKNEY SERIES."

AUSKERRY LIGHTHOUSE, STRONSAY, ORKNEY.

Left: It's obviously the same lighthouse and keepers' houses, but they have now been painted white to improve their effectiveness as a daymark. Its isolated and exposed position is seen to good effect in this view.

OUT SKERRIES

In March 1854 Britain went to war with Russia and the Admiralty in London decided that further navigation aids were required to ensure safe passage for the British fleet to and from Arctic waters along the north and east coasts of Shetland. At that time there were only three lighthouses covering both Orkney and Shetland.

The first light was a temporary structure established on 15th September 1854 on the island of Grunay, but the Board of Trade and Trinity House weren't happy and wanted a light established on Bound Skerry, a mile further east of Grunay but still within the Out Skerries group.

Thomas and David Stevenson built a permanent structure there between 1856–8 at a cost of £21,000 – 90% higher than their estimate! The tower is 98ft high giving it an elevation above high water of 132ft. Interestingly, the keepers' accommodation remained on Grunay, so Out Skerries lighthouse looks a lot like a pillar rock light planted on a low rocky islet because there are no buildings outside the tower itself. The station was made automatic and demanned from 7th April 1972.

During World War II the lighthouse buildings on Grunay were machine-gunned on 22nd February 1941 – exactly the same date as attacks on the Stroma and Pentland Skerries lights. Fortunately no one was injured. However, on Sunday, 18th January 1942 at 11.45am a single enemy bomber approached the island at low level from a westerly direction and passed directly over the lighthouse dwelling houses. One or two bombs were dropped, but they missed the buildings and fell into the sea. The plane circled and returned to drop another bomb which registered a direct hit on the boatman's house. The house was completely demolished and the sole occupant at the time, the boatman's mother, Mary Ann Anderson, was buried beneath the debris, sustaining injuries from which she died in Lerwick

on 20th January 1942. Further damage from this raid included the demolition of the boatman's wash house and coal cellar, and the keepers' cottages and outbuildings were either completely destroyed or badly damaged. Further evidence that even our most isolated lighthouses were not immune to the suffering and devastation of wartime Britain.

Below: A pillar rock tower planted on a rocky islet is exactly what the lighthouse at Out Skerries looks like. All the keepers' accommodation was on the island of Grunay – a mile away, but the lighthouse is actually on Bound Skerry. Out Skerries is the collective name for all the islands in the group.

Position:	North Sea, 20 mls NE of Lerwick, Shetland on Bound Skerry island
Constructed:	1856–58
Designer:	David & Thomas Stevenson
Builder:	David & Thomas Stevenson
Tower height:	98ft (30m)
Light character:	W Fl ev 20 secs
Range:	20 mls
Fog warning:	Discontinued
Automated:	April 1972

Skerries Lighthouse, Shetland

FAIR ISLE NORTH & SOUTH

North Lighthouse, Fair Isle

Fair Isle, home of the famous woollen sweater and shipping forecast sea area, is a small island, about 3 miles by 1½ miles, midway between Orkney and Shetland, although the island officially belongs to the Shetland group. It has two lighthouses, both established by David A. and Charles Stevenson in 1892. They are located at the northern and southern extremities of the island at the interestingly named locations of Skroo and Skaddan.

Even though they were built at the same time by the same engineers, they look quite different. The South light is virtually at sea level overlooking the South Harbour and has an 85ft tower with 96 steps to the lantern. Substantial keepers' houses were attached which have now become bed and breakfast accommodation. The North light sits on top of a sheer cliff 260ft above the sea, so it only needed a 47ft tower and 37 steps to the light. The former keepers' houses here were demolished after automation in 1983 and replaced with banks of solar panels to charge the batteries.

Fog is a particular weather problem for Fair Isle so both stations were equipped with foghorns, originally driven by compressed air but later by electricity. They were both discontinued, the one at the North light in October 2001, and the South light in June 2005 – when the last foghorn in Shetland became silent. The foghorn at the North light was some distance away from it, on the tip of a rocky promontory. To reach it involved a walk between two wire fences (that acted as handrails) and across an extremely exposed bridge that I imagine could only be described as 'exhilarating' in stormy conditions!

The Fair Isle lighthouses, just like the ones in Orkney, also attracted the unwanted attentions of enemy aircraft during World War II. The North lighthouse was seriously attacked twice. The first attack took place on 28th March 1941 when the

FAIR ISLE NORTH

Position:	North Sea, approx 25 mls SE of Sumburgh Head, Shetland
Constructed:	1892
Designer:	David A. & Charles Stevenson
Builder:	David A. & Charles Stevenson
Tower height:	47ft (15m)
Light character:	W Gp Fl (2) ev 30 secs
Range:	22 mls
Fog warning:	Discontinued 2001
Automated:	1983

Above: This is Skroo – the northernmost point of Fair Isle and the modest light here sits on top of a 200ft cliff. The sea is like a millpond in this hand-tinted card, not always the case around this lonely island. The walk to the fog horn – visible to the right of the tower on the cliff edge – could be a dangerous journey in wild weather. We can't quite see the exposed footbridge over a sheer drop in this card, or the flimsy wire handrails to cling on to in a storm.

dwelling houses were machine-gunned and two bombs dropped 60 yards from the lighthouse. The second attack happened on 18th April 1941. This time a single German plane machine-gunned and bombed the houses. One bomb scored a direct hit and caused great damage to the buildings, but no personnel were hurt in either of the attacks.

During an attack on the South light on 8th December 1941, Mrs Catherine Sutherland, wife of the assistant keeper was killed and their infant daughter slightly hurt. On 21st January 1942, Margaret Smith the wife of the principal keeper, and their 10 year-old daughter Margaret (Greta), were killed when the main dwelling block suffered a direct hit from a bomb. The building caught fire and was burned out. A 27 year-old anti-aircraft gunner stationed nearby, William Morris, was also killed in the same attack. Extensive damage was done to the station by fire, blast and flying debris.

Upon learning of the attack Roderick Macaulay, the assistant keeper at the North light, walked three miles through snowdrifts and storm to help restore the light at Fair Isle South. After this was achieved, he walked back in the dark to the North lighthouse to continue his duties there. For this deed he received a British Empire Medal for outstanding services. In March 1998, the Northern Lighthouse Board and Scotland's Lighthouse Museum erected a memorial plaque at Fair Isle South to those killed in these events. In the presence of HRH The Princess Royal, Patron of the Northern Lighthouse Board, the last keepers were withdrawn from Fair Isle South on 31st March 1998 marking the end of manned lighthouses in Scotland.

South Harbour, Fair Isle

Photo - J.D Ratter

Above: The lower elevation of the lighthouse at Fair Isle South meant a taller tower was needed to give the required range. This is the sheltered South Harbour at Skaddan and just above the boat is the landing stage where stores for the light were delivered. The area in front of the lighthouse is the site of Fair Isle's unique 6 hole golf course, built in 1960, that still exists today. Its fairways and greens are maintained by sheep and the weather, and play is suspended if a rare bird is spotted on the course!

FAIR ISLE SOUTH	
Position:	North Sea, approx 28 mls SE of Sumburgh Head, Shetland
Constructed:	1892
Designer:	David A. & Charles Stevenson
Builder:	David A. & Charles Stevenson
Tower height:	85ft (26m)
Light character:	W Gp Fl (4) ev 30 secs
Range:	22 mls
Fog warning:	Discontinued June 2005
Automated:	March 1998

MUCKLE FLUGGA

One of Britain's most famous and spectacular lighthouses sits on top of a pinnacle of rock called Muckle Flugga. It's the most northerly lighthouse in Britain and the rock it sits on is within a few hundred yards of being the most northern point of Britain before the Arctic Circle. The lighthouse was built as the direct result of a war, specifically the Crimean War, when the Commissioners for Northern Lighthouses were urged by the Government to erect a light at 'North Unst' – as Muckle Flugga was then known – to protect Her Majesty's ships on their way along the east coast of Shetland to blockade Russian ports.

Such was the urgency of their request that a temporary 50ft high tower with a cast iron lantern was said to have been completed in 26 days and lit on 11th October 1854. Only when you actually see the location of this light can you appreciate what a herculean task this must have been. Muckle Flugga is a razor-backed hump of rock that rises almost sheer on all sides to over 200ft above sea level. Everything needed for the construction of both the temporary and permanent lights had to be hauled up the sides of this rock from open boats.

It appears that the power of the sea at such a wild site was sadly underestimated with this first attempt. When waves climbed to the summit of the rock, knocked down walls, burst open the door to their accomodation and swept away water casks and anything else that wasn't firmly secured, the principal keeper, Mr Marchbanks, remarked that, "We had not a dry part to sit down in or even a dry bed to rest upon at night."

A more permanent brick structure was started in June 1855 by David Stevenson, 64ft high with walls 3½ ft thick and sunk 10ft into the summit of the rock. Bricks were chosen because they would be easier to land and transport from the smaller open boats to the summit of the rock. Compared with huge blocks of granite, the bricks could be thrown from the boat and caught by a labourer rather than requiring the use of a crane. Its light was first seen on 1st January 1858.

Although better than the original temporary light, life on Muckle Flugga was still pretty bleak for over a century. In 1968–69 a new dwelling block was built within the retaining wall in space saved by electrification, replacing the primitive conditions where another keeper claimed they 'slept in a crow's nest and ate in a cell'.

In the succeeding years Muckle Flugga has witnessed many storms of seismic fury, yet the light has continued in unbroken service. Every so often, the keepers reported instances of spectacular wave damage such as smashed lantern panes, pathways being swept away, or the materials stored in the courtyard being carried off by waves. In one winter storm, seas were reported to have been breaking over the rock for 21 hours continuously, during which time they swept away one gateway pillar and loosened the other. Huge blocks of stone, two feet square were described as being, 'rushed over the courtyard as if they had been wood'. There is even the story of a keeper

Previous page: Muckle Flugga in all its exposed, isolated glory at the edge of Britain. In this view we are looking north, which means the small lump of rock to the right is Out Stack, the very last piece of Britain before the Arctic Circle, and nearer to Bergen in Norway than Edinburgh. We can see that the lighthouse buildings are all enclosed inside a sturdy stone wall that suffered much torment and damage from winter storms. There's a flagpole in the yard and the bricks from which it has been built still remain unpainted.

Right: A lovely 1950s summer day at Muckle Flugga and perfect conditions for a relief if it was due. It's not clear in this card, which was taken from the cliff tops of Herma Ness on Unst, but between the lighthouse rock and the smaller one to its right, known as Little Flugga, there is a narrow 'gut' into which it's possible to ease a small boat to change keepers or deliver stores. The keepers then faced a leg-aching climb up 246 stone steps to the light while the stores were winched up on a 'blondin' wire. In recent years the slippery stone steps were replaced by flights of aluminium steps. We can see from this card that the image on the opposite page must have been taken by a photographer climbing to the comparatively flat top of the next rock called Cliff Skerry with his camera and tripod – but without the aid of steps. As we have seen on previous occasions in this book, and will continue to see later on, early postcard photographers were an intrepid bunch who would not hesitate to take some degree of risk to get their shot.

Left: This card has been copied from an earlier engraving that featured a tall sailing ship on the horizon – which has been replaced by the steam ship in this view. Like the original, this card has been painted by someone who has probably never seen Muckle Flugga – or North Unst as it was known in 1909 when it was posted. The tower is obviously too tall, and the rock itself has been exaggerated to Matterhorn proportions, but it does convey something of the lighthouse's dramatic isolation.

finding a live fish in one of the summit pools – at an elevation of over 50ft higher than Nelson's Column!

The last keepers were lifted from the Muckle Flugga helipad on 20th March 1995 and in so doing left Britain's most northerly permanently inhabited island to the wind and the waves once more.

Position:	North Sea, 1 ml N of Unst, Shetland
Constructed:	1854–58
Designer:	David & Thomas Stevenson
Builder:	David & Thomas Stevenson, and Alan Brebner
Tower height:	64ft (20m)
Light character:	W Gp Fl (2) ev 20 secs
Range:	22 mls
Fog warning:	None
Automated:	March 1995

SULE SKERRY

Left: A really crisp real photograph card of Sule Skerry from about 1912 showing the basic conditions the keepers endured at Britain's most isolated lighthouse. At the top of the tower is a massive lantern containing a huge hyper-radial optic to give an increased range to its flash. A shaft of sunlight has caught some of the panes of glass in the lantern emphasising the traditional triangular shape of the windows. There is obviously a fire burning in the building on the left, and surrounding the base of the tower are a series of what appear to be store rooms. A keeper is just visible in front of the door of one.

There aren't many British lighthouses that are so isolated they can't be seen from the nearest landfall. Sule Skerry is not only one of them, but until its automation in December 1982 it held the impressive distinction of being the most isolated manned British lighthouse of all – further from civilisation than any other lighthouse around the coasts of England, Wales or Scotland. Only vessels in the Pentland Firth on passage to or from the north Atlantic are likely to pass close enough to spot it.

The lighthouse is in the centre of a small island, 35 acres in area and just 45ft above sea level that rises 40 miles west of Orkney and 45 miles north west of Dunnet Head, Caithness. The centre of the island is covered with a thin, sandy soil, but there's absolutely nothing else on Sule Skerry – apart from thousands and thousands of puffins and seals. One of the first keepers of the lighthouse was astonished by exactly how many puffins arrived at Sule Skerry during the summer, 'The air is black with them, the ground is covered with them, and the sea is alive with them', he noted.

Its isolation meant that it took the three years from 1892–94 for David A. Stevenson and his brother Charles to build a lighthouse on Sule Skerry. The exceptionally fine summer of 1893 saw completion of the 89ft high tower topped with a huge lantern, followed next year by internal fixtures and fittings and a tramway to carry heavy and bulky goods from the landing place to the tower. Winter work was ruled out by the short day length and stormy weather preventing delivery of materials and safe working.

Lighting it was delayed for a year while the Board of Trade and Trinity House argued with the Commissioners about the cost and character of the lens apparatus. Its lantern was bigger than any other previously seen in the lighthouse service – 16ft in diameter compared to the normal 12ft – to accommodate a huge hyper-radial lens. This had more powerful oil burners at the heart of the lantern and the increased heat generated required a larger diameter for the cage of glass that revolved around them for its dissipation. Also, an arrangement of equi-angular prisms invented by Charles Stevenson reduced the loss of light and divergence compared to other lens designs, and gave the lighthouse a much greater range – a vital requirement for such an isolated beacon. The new light, first seen in 1895, was observed from Cape Wrath, 35 miles away, on 60 evenings during the first three months.

Communication was always going to be a problem at this site, particularly as the keepers' families lived in Stromness, Orkney since it was first built. Sule Skerry was no place to raise a family. Pigeon post was tried as a means of communication but was not successful as some of the birds were allegedly shot at (for food) on their return to the loft in Stromness. The lack of sun also hindered an experiment with a heliograph made by assistant lightkeeper James Tomison.

Since Sule Skerry was built, it has of course lost its keepers to automation – as has every other British lighthouse. It can no longer claim to be our most isolated manned light – because no such structure now exists. In the meantime the Northern Lighthouse Board has built several new modern beacons on equally isolated islands such as North Rona and Sula Sgeir. Although they were planned as unmanned beacons from the start, their remoteness is such that had they been built a century earlier as lighthouses by a member of the Stevenson family, then it is one of these islands that would probably have claimed the most isolated British lighthouse record.

Suleskerry Lighthouse

2.5.8.51 ⓙⓥ

Above: This hand-tinted view of Sule Skerry lighthouse from 1910 was probably taken from a relief vessel standing off the island and, if nothing else, emphasises the bleakness of the location. Nowhere does Sule Skerry get higher than 45ft above sea level and the only plants that can survive are those tough enough to withstand ferocious winds and nesting puffins. There are no trees!

Position:	Atlantic Ocean, 37 mls NE of Cape Wrath, Highland
Constructed:	1892–95
Designer:	David A. Stevenson
Builder:	David A. & Charles Stevenson
Tower height:	89ft (27m)
Light character:	W Gp Fl (2) ev 15 secs
Range:	21 mls
Fog warning:	None
Automated:	December 1982

FLANNAN ISLES

The Flannan Isles are a lonely cluster of seven uninhabited islands – sometimes known as the Seven Hunters – 20 miles further west than the Outer Hebrides and over 80 miles from the Scottish mainland. The largest is Eilean Mor, and on its summit is a lighthouse built by David A. Stevenson between 1895–99 as a landfall light for vessels crossing the Atlantic and approaching Britain from the west. With an elevation of 285ft its light was visible for an impressive 25 miles.

Even though it was isolated, its construction wasn't particularly problematical. The contractor was George Lawson of Rutherglen whose tender of £6,914 1s 9d included the building of the landing places and stairs, etc on Eilean Mor. Mr Lawson also built the dwelling houses for the lightkeepers' wives and families at the shore station at Breasclete, Isle of Lewis, which cost another £3,526 16s 0d. The site for the shore station was chosen for its close proximity to Loch Roag, a sea loch that provided a safe anchorage and shelter for the lighthouse tender when bad weather made it impossible to carry out the relief on the due date.

There was no radio communication between the Flannans and Lewis at that time, so a gamekeeper, Mr Roderick MacKenzie, was appointed as 'observer' to the light, for which he received payment of £8 per annum. His duties involved watching for any signals from the lighthouse 18 miles north-west of his vantage point on Gallan Head, Lewis and to observe and report any failure in the exhibition of the light. In the event of such a failure he was required to report it immediately by telegram to the NLB in Edinburgh.

Little did anyone know on 7th December 1899 when the lighthouse was first lit, how soon the lighthouse tender in Loch Roag and the observer at Gallan Head would play their part in one of the most famous sea mysteries in the world, and one that has never been satisfactorily resolved.

The lighthouse was only just over a year old when, in December 1900, a series of events unfolded on the Flannan Isles that resulted in the disappearance, for an unknown reason, of all three lighthouse keepers. Their bodies were never found and the few clues remaining on the island have never been able to conclusively prove what happened to the three men. It remains to this day the 'Mary Celeste' of the lighthouse world.

The mystery of the Flannan Isles lighthouse is a well-told story than can be summarised briefly as follows. Ten days before Christmas a passing steamer from America failed to spot the flash it knew should be visible from the Flannan Isles lighthouse and reported it after docking at Oban. Poor visibility meant that the observer at Gallan Head couldn't tell whether the lighthouse was operational or not. The lighthouse tender in Loch Roag was due to relieve the keepers on 20th December but a series of gales prevented her leaving until the 26th. No signs of life were found on the island – all three keepers had disappeared

Flannan Islands Lighthouse, Scotland.
Light is White, Group Flashing, 434,000 C. Power visible 24 miles.

Flannen Islands Light, Hebrides Islands, Scotland.
Light, White, Group Flashing, visible 24 miles,

Position:	Atlantic Ocean, 18 mls W of Lewis, Outer Hebrides
Constructed:	1895–99
Designer:	David A. Stevenson
Builder:	George Lawson
Tower height:	75ft (23m)
Light character:	W Gp Fl (2) ev 30 secs
Range:	20 mls
Fog warning:	None
Automated:	September 1971

Previous page: Both these cards were produced by the Lighthouse Literature Mission who always printed some technical details about the light on the front of their cards. This card was posted in 1910, just ten years after the three keepers disappeared in mysterious circumstances. Their three replacements can be seen as silhouettes to the left of the lighthouse door.

Above: Another card from the same publisher, but this one has its location misspelt as 'Flannen'. The three keepers look to be posing for the photographer with some satisfaction as they have undoubtedly used every flag in the flag locker to display from the flag pole. It could be that an annual inspection visit from one of the Commissioners was due and this was a form of welcome.

– and entries in the logbook clearly showed that all was well until the afternoon of 15th December. The clues left behind such as a knocked-over chair, a partly-prepared meal, and the ownership of the waterproof clothing left on its peg, have all contributed to a sea mystery that still has no satisfactory explanation.

An investigation was conducted and official reports were prepared which seemed to suggest that the most likely explanation was that two of the keepers left the lighthouse in deteriorating weather conditions to secure ropes and equipment on the west landing stage that was set in a deep gulley or geo at the bottom of many flights of steps. The third keeper continued to prepare their meal until he noticed some unusually large swells approaching from the west. He knew that the funnelling effect of the gully in which the men were working could be exceptionally dangerous in westerly gales and left the lighthouse in a hurry, without waterproof clothing, to run to the landing stage to warn them of the approaching danger. As he arrived the swells filled the gully and swept all three keepers into the sea. But the truth is, nobody knows for sure what really happened, although many alternative fanciful theories have been put forward.

The lighthouse was given three new keepers and continued to flash its warning from 26th December 1900 until a comparatively early automation in September 1971. It was converted to use acetylene gas, and later still in 1999 its power was produced by solar panels and wind generators.

For many schoolchildren the events here are dramatically described in W.W. Gibson's 1912 poem *The Flannan Isles* which contains the final verse, 'We seem'd to stand for an endless while, Though still no word was said, Three men alive on Flannan Isle, Who thought on three men dead'.

MONACH ISLES

The Monach Isles are five low-lying islands about four miles west of North Uist in the Outer Hebrides. The westernmost island of the group is Shillay and the location of the Monachs lighthouse. Early records reveal that monks had a monastery on Shillay that gave rise to its Gaelic name of Eilean nam Manach – the island of the monks.

Because of its strategic position on the west coast of the Outer Hebrides, Shillay was bought for £400 in 1862 by the Northern Lighthouse Board who had David and Thomas Stevenson build a rather impressive 133ft high red brick lighthouse there two years later. It cost £14,673 and the light was first exhibited on 1st February 1864. The name 'Monach Isles' was chosen for the station over the local name, Heisgeir, to avoid confusion with Hasgeir to the north, and even another Hyskeir, off Canna, (see next page) which was also to receive a lighthouse 40 years after Monach.

The light was closed down in 1942 during the war. At the end of hostilities in 1945 it was not relit and in 1948, after extensive enquiries had been made from shipping, it was considered that the light had ceased to be of value to general navigation. On 22nd November 1948 it was therefore permanently discontinued. This, however, is not the end of the story.

Nearly 50 years later, in July 1996, the NLB received approval and finance from the Department of Transport for the construction of three new lighthouses to mark the Deep Water Route, west of the Hebrides. This route was recommended for laden tankers in Lord Donaldson's Report, *Safer Ships, Cleaner Seas*, which followed the 1993 *Braer* disaster in the Shetlands. One of the new minor lights was destined for the Monachs. It was a square, solar-powered and white metal-clad tower 26ft high, built between April and October 1997 just a short distance from the base of the original tower.

There is an unusual postscript to the Monachs lighthouse story. In 2005 following a review of marine aids to navigation carried out by the General Lighthouse Authorities it was decided to increase the range of the Monach Isles light from 10 to 18 miles. To achieve the extra range the light would have to be raised, but the design of the existing 1997 lighthouse was not suitable for the increased height required. Also, a rotating light, with a larger array of solar panels and increased battery capacity was considered the best option for its increased status as a major light. This was achieved by housing a new optic in the original 1864 lighthouse tower. The new elevation of the light of 153ft meant its light would be visible for 18 miles. On 25th July 2008 the Northern Lighthouse Board issued a Notice to Mariners stating, 'the existing light will be discontinued and a new light will be established in the former lighthouse tower'.

This means that the island of Shillay has gone from having no light, to a major light, back to no light, to a minor light and finally back to a major light again over a period of almost 150 years. A remarkable achievement!

Position:	Atlantic Ocean, 7 mls NW of South Uist, Outer Hebrides
Constructed:	1864
Designer:	David & Thomas Stevenson
Builder:	David & Thomas Stevenson
Tower height:	133ft (41m)
Light character:	W Gp Fl (2) ev 15 secs
Range:	18 mls
Fog warning:	None
Automated:	July 2008

Below: Postcards of the Monach Isles lighthouse are quite rare – this is the only one I've ever seen. An isolated location off the west coast of the Outer Hebrides, and the fact that they are uninhabited has no doubt reduced the market for such a card. The lighthouse itself is a substantial structure with a huge brick tower, and one that the NLB can justifiably claim to have made full use of. The light was discontinued in 1948 and 60 years later it was reinstated in the same tower – recycling at its best!

Monach Lighthouse Hebrides Island, Scotland

HYSKEIR

The stretch of water that separates the Inner and Outer Hebrides is known as the Sea of the Hebrides. The further north you travel up the Sea of the Hebrides the narrower it gets, until it becomes The Little Minch. At the point where the narrowing begins lie the islands of Rum, Eigg, Muck and Canna and to the south west of this cluster we find a small island of 40 acres known as Oigh-sgeir, or more commonly Hyskeir, upon which sits the rather elegant Hyskeir lighthouse.

Both Hyskeir and Canna are comparatively low-lying compared to the neighbouring Rum, and were therefore quite difficult to spot at sea level from a distance. The light on Hyskeir was built to warn of both islands and also a dangerous outlying clump called Mills Rocks.

After the NLB had bought the island in 1902 for £611 3s 3d David Alan Stevenson designed the light – a slender tower 128ft high (with 155 steps to the top) that gave a range of almost 30 miles. It cost £15,134 and was first lit in 1904.

From the very beginning the lighthouse was considered a rock station with the keepers' families living away on shore. However, instead of building their homes on the nearest landfall, which was the usual arrangement, they were purpose-built on Pulpit Hill in Oban where keepers from Barra Head and Skerryvore lighthouses also came to live at a later date.

In its later years, when the NLB were experimenting with helicopters to change keepers in the early 1970s, Hyskeir was one of the first stations chosen to experience the benefits of this method of relief, but the heavy items such as oil and equipment still had to be landed by the lighthouse tender. During the winter of 1980, bad weather had prevented the lighthouse vessel *Fingal* from delivering ten barrels of oil on a number of occasions between September and January. When the supplies were finally landed, only two days supply of oil were left at the station. A close call!

Hyskeir also became well-known amongst the lighthouse community for its one-hole golf course, and also for the immaculate vegetable garden that was maintained by the keepers. All this came to an end in March 1997 when Hyskeir was the last rock station in Britain to be automated and the keepers were finally withdrawn, leaving the island once more to the terns, eider ducks and grey seals.

Position:	Sea of the Hebrides, 33 mls W of Mallaig, Highland
Constructed:	1904
Designer:	David A. Stevenson
Builder:	David A. Stevenson
Tower height:	128ft (39m)
Light character:	W Gp Fl (3) ev 30 secs
Range:	24 mls
Fog warning:	Discontinued
Automated:	March 1997

Below: Another Lighthouse Literature Mission card, of Hyskeir lighthouse. Most of the technical details carried by these cards are still correct – its position, the height of the tower, and often the flash characteristics. But the candle power and range of the light are usually the ones they possessed when first built or the card was issued, and therefore don't reflect current specifications.

Hyskeir Lighthouse, West Coast of Scotland.
Tower 128 feet high.
Light Group Flashing, White. Visible 17 miles.

BARRA HEAD

Barra Head Lighthouse, Scotland.
Tower is 60 feet high, but owing to position on cliffs, Light is 683 feet above high water.
Light is white, occulting, visible 33 miles.

Position:	Atlantic Ocean, W end of Berneray, Outer Hebrides
Constructed:	1830–33
Designer:	Robert Stevenson
Builder:	Robert Stevenson
Tower height:	59ft (18m)
Light character:	W Fl ev 15 secs
Range:	18 mls
Fog warning:	None
Automated:	October 1980

Above: Yet another Lighthouse Literature Mission card with its distinctive embossed border and technical details – correct when the lighthouse was built but navigational technology has changed and so has Barra Head's characteristic flash. Its range then was 33 miles – now it's just 18.

The single-storey keepers' accommodation and modest tower were all constructed from granite and designed to resist the unimaginable wind speeds experienced at its wild cliff top location. We can see three metal tanks against the outside wall. These were for the collection of rainwater – fresh water was a precious commodity at such a height.

Barra Head lighthouse is another remarkable piece of Stevenson engineering, and unusual because it is named after an island many miles away from where it is actually situated.

The Outer Hebrides archipelago finally peters out on an island called Berneray, modest in area but mighty in elevation. The cliffs on its western edge rise vertically out of the Atlantic to over 600ft, and at a promontory known as Sron an Duin Robert Stevenson built a lighthouse between 1830–33 with a modest granite tower just 59ft tall. He called it Barra Head lighthouse (after the island of that name 15 miles to the north) but on the top of such huge cliffs the elevation of the lantern was 693ft above sea level – making it the highest lighthouse in Britain. However, such elevation also brought with it the problem of fog, and this light was also considered to be the most fog-bound of all NLB lights. The situation was so bad that hot water pipes were installed to heat the lantern in winter.

Robert Stevenson had earmarked this island as a site for a possible light when he toured the west coast of Scotland in 1829. Its strategic position at the southern entrance to The Minch would not only assist local shipping but also those approaching the west coast of Scotland from the Atlantic. It wasn't a particularly difficult project to construct, apart from the fact that the only landing on the island was 1¼ miles away and everything needed to build it had to be hauled across the boggy moorland and from sea level up to 600ft. The oil burning light was first exhibited on the night of 15th October 1833.

Berneray is a bleak and inhospitable place, but nevertheless traces of Neolithic, Bronze Age, Iron Age and Norse settlement have been found. In 1851 Berneray's Roman Catholic population had reached 28 but by 1910 they had all gone – apart

BARRA HEAD LIGHTHOUSE, (580 FT) HIGHEST IN BRITISH ISLES.

Left: There's little sense in this delightful sepia card of Barra Head's exposed position. We can't see the 600ft cliff face that is on the far side of the lighthouse, and the track that is zig-zagging its way up to the tower through a set of imposing gateposts has come from the island's only landing place over a mile away.

Apart from the fact that the lighthouse buildings and tower have now been painted white, there are no obvious clues to the date of this card. However, postcard collectors know that Valentines – who produced this card – always put a code number on every card, which can be dated. The 224544 in the left hand corner means this card was taken in 1934.

from the three lighthouse keepers. The stone cross on the main elevation of the keepers' houses makes Barra Head the only Scottish lighthouse to feature a cross. Close to the lighthouse is a walled graveyard in which there are headstones to Catharine Black and Alexander McIntosh both died aged two years, and a daughter and son of the Reid family.

The weather at this extremity of the British Isles could, as you might imagine, be extremely violent. Between the elegant keepers' cottages (which apparently would not have looked out of place in Edinburgh's New Town) and the lighthouse tower was a cobbled courtyard. During some of the worst winter storms it was said to be almost impossible to walk across, and into it fish were sometimes blown!

In 1831 Robert Stevenson himself wrote that, 'Such is the violence of the wind in this station from the lofty and abrupt form of the island that the temporary buildings occupied by the artificers engaged in the works had been temporarily unroofed. On the face of precipitous cliffs of 645' in height on which the lighthouse stands exposed to the whole fetch of the Western ocean, the winds and seas acquire a force which the reporter has never experienced elsewhere. The artificers are often reduced to the necessity of passing the most exposed places on their knees clinging with their hands to the ground in going to and from their barracks … In one of these storms the lighthouse cart and horse were overturned by the force of the wind. Both shafts were broken and the body of the cart was disengaged and carried into the air 15' or 20' from the ground while the wheels ran down the clopping bank for some distance. It is remarkable that the horse sustained no injury'.

It was probably during one of these ferocious tempests after the last war that a Blenheim bomber crashed into the cliff face close to the lighthouse and no one heard it. By identifying the markings and parts from the aircraft when it was eventually found, the crew could be identified.

Barra Head lighthouse was converted to automatic operation, and the last inhabitants of Berneray were finally withdrawn, on 23rd October 1980. Advancing technology means that the light can be switched on and off by a sun valve. The main optic is an acetylene-operated Dalen lamp, and the rotating Fresnel lens equipment gives 1 flash every 15 seconds with a range of 18 miles.

AILSA CRAIG

Ailsa Craig, The Lighthouse.

Ailsa Craig (often referred to as 'Paddy's Milestone') is a huge conical lump of granite and basalt – the plug of a 500 million-year-old volcano – that rises to 1,114ft out of the Firth of Clyde 10 miles west of Girvan. It drops almost vertically into the sea and is virtually impossible to land on, apart from one area on its eastern flank called Foreland Point. This is where Thomas and David A. Stevenson built a lighthouse between 1882–86.

The island is regularly plagued by fog and sea mists, sometimes just a wispy cap, but frequently down to sea level obscuring the whole island. This produced petitions in 1881 to the Commissioners of Northern Lighthouses from Lloyds and the Scottish Shipmasters Association requesting the erection of two fog signals and a lighthouse on Ailsa Craig. The Board of Trade and Trinity House both agreed and work commenced the following year. The light was first exhibited from the top of a 36ft tower on the night of 15th June 1886, a paraffin-burning light that remained in use until 24th January 1911, when it was converted to an incandescent lamp.

The fog signals were sirens erected on the north and south ends of the island, two huge concrete horn houses with a metal horn projecting from them. Gas engines in a central gasworks powered them until 1911, when they were replaced by oil-driven engines. These were permanently discontinued in November 1966, and replaced by a Tyfon compressed air fog signal, which had a character of three blasts, each of three seconds duration every 45 seconds. It was sounded from a position close to the lighthouse and not at either of the previous fog siren sites. This in turn was discontinued in 1987.

Until wireless telephone communications were established on Ailsa Craig in 1935, the lightkeepers and employees of Ailsa Craig

Position:	Firth of Clyde, 10 mls W of Girvan, Dumfries & Galloway
Constructed:	1882–86
Designer:	David A. & Thomas Stevenson
Builder:	David A. & Thomas Stevenson
Tower height:	36ft (11m)
Light character:	W Fl ev 4 secs
Range:	17 mls
Fog warning:	Discontinued
Automated:	March 1990

Above: It looks like all three keepers and their families have assembled on the lantern gallery of Ailsa Craig lighthouse. Difficult to be sure, but I think I can count at least nine people assembled for this group photo. A couple of keepers can be picked out by their characteristic NLB caps, and several of the ladies have their best hats on. We'll probably never know if there was any special significance in having this photograph taken.

Granites Ltd used to depend on pigeons for the conveyance of messages. A pigeon house was established on Girvan Green in 1935. The pigeons were provided by the lighthouse boatman in return for an annual payment of £4. The birds, of course, could only fly in reasonable conditions, so when a doctor or supplies were required urgently in stormy weather a system of fire signals was used. One fire on the path leading from the lighthouse to the castle meant 'bring a doctor for the Lighthouse'; two fires on the same path meant 'bring a doctor for the Quarry Company'; one fire on the Castle Flat to the north of the lighthouse indicated 'provisions are required'.

The granite company became famous for extracting a particular rare type of granite known as 'ailsite' that was used to make curling stones, including the ones used by the Scottish Women's Curling Team and Winter 2002 Olympic Gold medal winners.

The lighthouse was automated in 1990 and is now remotely monitored from the Northern Lighthouse Board's offices in Edinburgh. The tower is listed as being of architectural interest, and in 2001 as part of the NLB's solarisation programme banks of solar panels were erected on the roof of the former keepers' cottages and the station was converted to solar-electric power. It shows one white flash every four seconds that is visible for 17 miles – enough for the reassuring light to be seen from the sea front at Girvan, weather permitting!

Right: The lighthouse was built on the only flat space large enough for it on the whole island, at Foreland Point on its east coast. It sits inside its own walled enclosure and behind it rises the huge bulk of Ailsa Craig itself. The island was a popular day trip for tourists who could buy postcards and have them franked with a special 'Ailsa Craig' postmark, as this 1925 card has been, to verify that they had actually set foot upon it.

Below: An early 1900s view showing Foreland Point and the back of the lighthouse. To get the tourists to Ailsa involved the construction of a couple of wooden jetties so the Clyde steamers could disembark their passengers at any state of the tide. There were even tea rooms on the island to refresh the visitors before their journey home.

THE LIGHTHOUSE STATION, AILSA CRAIG

Ailsa Craig Lighthouse and Quay

PLADDA

Pladda is a pear-shaped island, about a mile off Kildonan on the south-east corner of Arran. When there was such a person as a lighthouse keeper, the three employed at Ailsa Craig could check on the correct operation of the lighthouse on Pladda, and vice versa because they were only 12 miles apart. In 1790, when Pladda was constructed, it was only the fifth lighthouse in Scotland.

Towards the end of the eighteenth century Scottish sea trade was booming. It was estimated that the port of Greenock was handling several hundred ships daily carrying mainly tobacco and cotton from the Americas. Each one had to pick its way up the Firth of Clyde – by no means easy when the fog was down. A general clamour for more lights along the Firth produced an Act of Parliament in 1789 for the Northern Lighthouse Board to erect a light on Pladda. Thomas Smith was the engineer and George Shiells the mason in charge. Its 95ft stone tower was completed within a year and first lit on 1st October 1790.

However, it wasn't long before Smith was back on Pladda to erect a second smaller tower, 43ft high, in front of the original. Both showed fixed white lights but Pladda's two fixed white lights were invaluable in distinguishing them from others that were visible in the Clyde approaches.

In 1870 trials were carried out at Pladda using paraffin as an illuminant. It was a light mineral oil that eventually superseded colza, just as colza had succeeded sperm oil. After its introduction became widespread the nickname for a Scottish lighthouse keeper became a 'paraffin oiler'. By 1901 its two fixed lights were no longer regarded as suitable for the great landfall and coastal lights and a powerful group flashing light was installed instead.

Boatmen permanently attached to the station, who also carried out the reliefs, brought provisions and other stores to the lighthouse. These attending

PLADDA LIGHTHOUSE, KILDONAN, ARRAN.

boats were limited to four visits to the rock per month, and two on Sundays to enable the lightkeepers to attend church. This lasted until 1972 with the introduction of helicopter reliefs, followed in 1990, two centuries after it first showed its light, by automation. Pladda once again has no permanent inhabitants.

Position:	Firth of Clyde, 1½ mls S of Isle of Arran, Strathclyde
Constructed:	1789–90
Designer:	Thomas Smith
Builder:	George Shiells
Tower height:	95ft (29m)
Light character:	W Gp Fl (3) ev 30 secs
Range:	17 mls
Fog warning:	Discontinued
Automated:	March 1990

Previous page: A hand-tinted card from about 1910 showing a very tranquil scene at Pladda. Sheep graze in front of the lighthouse flagpole while to the left are the red-bricked keepers' cottages. At the time this card was produced, the lighthouse was already a century old. From this angle it appears to have just a single tower.

Left: If we move around the lighthouse from the previous card and view it from seaward, the unique double-tower arrangement at Pladda becomes apparent in this 1905 card. The taller tower with its two lantern galleries is the original 1790 light, and the smaller tower in front of it was added a few years later to give Pladda two fixed white lights. The foghorn building has two horns projecting from it on different faces to warn of the frequent fogs that form in the Firth of Clyde. A sizeable crowd has gathered in front of the light, probably not the keepers and their families as most of them appear to be ladies in hats, more likely to be a party of day trippers from Kildonan on Arran.

Below: A lovely card from the late 1950s that shows the relationship between Arran (where the photographer is standing), the island of Pladda (on the right), and the triangular bulk of Ailsa Craig on the horizon.

Pladda Lighthouse, Kildonan, Isle of Arran.

KILDONAN, ISLE OF ARRAN, SHOWING PLADDA LIGHTHOUSE AND AILSA CRAIG.   B.3058.

SANDA

Sanda Lighthouse.

Left: Sanda's lighthouse sits on top of the huge bulk of Ship Rock with its dramatic natural arch. Stevenson's unique solution to its Muckle Flugga-like elevation was to construct two enclosed staircases each with circular battlements and attractive windows to get the keepers from almost sea level to the summit of the rock. To reach the lantern meant the keepers climbing these two towers then the stairs inside the lighthouse tower itself – a total of 210 steps!

Opposite page: From this angle we can also see the keepers' cottages on the left, and the clever way that Stevenson integrated the two giant stairwells into the fabric of the rock. The high white stone wall would have offered the keepers a small measure of protection against the ferocious winds that swept through the gap between the lighthouse rock and their cottages, before they started a leg-aching climb to the lantern.

Sanda lighthouse is situated on a small private island, just half a square mile in area, off the southern tip of the Mull of Kintyre. It marks the turning for vessels into the Clyde after passing through the North Channel between Scotland and Ireland. There is a small population on the island who provide boat trips and self-catering accommodation for visitors. It is a favourite port of call for yachts and a Site of Special Scientific Interest. Legend has it that St Ninian himself is buried on Sanda (Norse, *Sandy Island*) and that death within a year will fall upon anyone who stands on his grave.

When the *Christiana*, outward bound from

Glasgow in bad weather, was lost with all hands on the nearby Pattersons Rock in 1825, renewed demands for a light on this island were made to Trinity House – who at that time had to sanction all new lighthouse construction around British coasts, even in Scotland. They in turn proposed to the Commissioners of Northern Lighthouses that the light of the Mull of Kintyre should be moved to Sanda! The Commissioners declined, although they were willing to mark Pattersons Rock with a beacon.

However, as wrecks continued, they later decided to build on the summit of the Ship Rock – a small promontory on Sanda's south coast. In fact it's often

Position:	Firth of Clyde, 2½ mls S of Mull of Kintyre, Argyll & Bute
Constructed:	1850
Designer:	Alan Stevenson
Builder:	Alan Stevenson
Tower height:	64ft (20m)
Light character:	W Fl (1) ev 10 secs
Range:	15 mls
Fog warning:	Discontinued
Automated:	March 1992

referred to as the Ship lighthouse. Alan Stevenson, its engineer, built a stone tower on the top of the rock that was accessed by two enclosed sets of steps built against the landward face of the rock. It was a unique design, still the only one of its kind, from the same engineer who had put a lighthouse on Skerryvore six years previously. It was first lit in 1850.

It was close to Sanda lighthouse that the NLB lost one of its own ships. The *Signal* had the misfortune to run aground on the Mull of Kintyre peninsula in dense fog in 1895 en route from McArthur's Head to Sanda. The boats were launched and all on board, including one of the Commissioners, Sheriff William Ivory, were saved with most of their effects. Attempts to salvage the ship proved fruitless, and she sank the next day.

There have been further notable shipwrecks around Sanda. The largest was on 17th March 1946 when the 7000-tonne American liberty ship *Byron Darnton* ran aground in dense fog 100 yards south-west of the lighthouse on the return leg of her maiden voyage. The 54 passengers and crew on board and all were saved by the Campbeltown lifeboat. In 2003 the ship gave its name to a newly-opened public house on the island – said to be the most remote public house in the British Isles.

Less fortunate was the Dutch cattle ship *Hereford Express* that went aground on Sanda on 19th October 1970. Her cargo of livestock were either drowned or destroyed by the SSPCA officers who flew out to Sanda by helicopter.

In 1953 Sanda lighthouse was classified as a rock station and the families were moved to the mainland. The keepers were then relieved by boat, but in 1976/77 helicopter reliefs were introduced from Campbeltown. On 26th March 1992 the final keepers left the island as automation took over and arrays of solar panels and back-up diesel generators appeared. Although wind generators are commonplace at other automated lighthouses they have failed to survive Sanda's wild winters where wind speeds are estimated 'to have exceeded 200mph'! This is probably a slight exaggeration although the damage done by the wind at such an exposed station as Sanda is not.

The former keepers' cottages are now used for self-catering holiday accommodation, and in 1996 the surprised occupants of one of them opened their door to Her Royal Highness The Princess Royal, Patron of the Northern Lighthouse Board who was visiting Sanda lighthouse and popped in for a cup of tea!

The 2001 census confirmed that Sanda was one of only four Scottish islands with a population of one person. This soon soared by 200% – to 3. In August 2008 the island was put up for sale by the owner at a a price of £3.2 million.

SANDA LIGHTHOUSE.

878 / 12

THE SKERRIES

The Skerries, a low lying cluster of rocks four miles off the northern coast of Anglesey and directly in the path of shipping from Liverpool to Ireland, is an interesting station in the history of British lighthouses. Not so much for its difficulty of construction, but more for the complex legal wranglings that eventually brought it under the control of Trinity House.

Henry Hascard, a private speculator who saw the lucrative possibilities of the tolls that could be levied on the site, offered to build a light on the Skerries as long ago as 1658. Trinity House, jealously guarding their rights in a Charter of 1566 that gave them the sole right to supervise the erection of lighthouses and beacons, rejected his offer, as was a subsequent petition in 1705 from a Captain John Davison. But by 1714 things were becoming more urgent for some kind of sea mark on the Skerries and William Trench, who actually held the lease of the Skerries, was granted a patent by Queen Anne for the building of a light.

For a Crown Rent of £5 a year, Trench had the right to levy dues of 1d per ship and 2d per ton of cargo. However, this turned out to be far from being the profitable venture that he envisaged, and the Skerries eventually proved to be his downfall.

When the primitive coal-fired grate on top of a 36ft stone tower light was first kindled on 4th November 1717 it was the first permanent light along the entire west coast of England. William Trench used to be a wealthy landowner, but the estimated £3,000 construction cost, the price of 100 tons of coal every year and the fact that traders and mariners evaded payment of dues caused him to fall heavily into debt. He died in 1729 a ruined man.

After Trench's death the lease passed to his daughter Anne and her husband Sutton Morgan, and because of the nature of the debt, an Act of Parliament was passed in 1730 to give his family sole claim to the Skerries light dues in perpetuity. This act subsequently caused a great deal of embarrassment to Trinity House.

In 1834 when an attempt was made to purchase the patent for this lighthouse, its new proprietor, Morgan Jones, asserted that under this Act he was absolved from any responsibility to sell. For five years after the Act of 1836 that empowered Trinity House to purchase all remaining private lighthouses, he opposed the purchase, during which time the increase in sea trade into and out of Liverpool made the Skerries an extremely profitable light. It was finally purchased by Trinity House in 1841 for £444,984, the last privately-owned lighthouse in the British Isles to be bought by Trinity House and it cost them an absolute fortune to do so.

Since it was originally built, the coal-burning grate – once described as one of the worst lights in the United Kingdom – was replaced in 1804 by an oil lamp, and in 1846 the whole station was enlarged and improved by Trinity House's James Walker to give it the appearance it has today. Electricity arrived in 1927 and automation in 1987, ending a period of 270 years of continuous manned service.

SKERRIES LIGHTHOUSE FROM THE AIR

Skerries Lighthouse.

Opposite page: From the air it becomes obvious just what a hazard to shipping the Skerries reef was – a low-lying jumble of rocks in the direct path of vessels making to or from Liverpool. The present lighthouse sits on the highest point on the reef, and in this 1951 card we can also see the walled garden where the keepers were able to grow an extensive range of fresh vegetables to supplement the stores delivered by boat.

Left: This is an earlier hand-coloured card of James Walker's impressive 1846 light on the Skerries that replaced a particularly ineffective coal-burning grate from William Trench. We can see that the wall of the walled garden was quite a substantial structure that offered much protection to the well-tended vegetables inside. Sadly, when helicopter reliefs started in the 1970s a large proportion of the wall and garden disappeared to make room for a helipad.

Position:	Irish Sea, 7 mls NE of Holyhead, Anglesey
Constructed:	1714–17, 1803–04
Designer:	William Trench, James Walker
Builder:	William Trench, James Walker
Tower height:	36ft (12m), 75ft (23m)
Light character:	Coal fire, W Gp Fl (2) ev 10 secs
Range:	Unknown, 22 mls
Fog warning:	Electric (2) ev 20 secs
Automated:	September 1987

BARDSEY ISLAND

VIS 17 MILES

F.H.MAY.COPYRIGHT.

BARDSEY ISLAND LIGHTHOUSE. N.W

Left: An undated sepia card showing the elegant square tower design of Joseph Nelson's 1821 lighthouse with its red and white bands. 'Vis 17 miles' refers to the range of the light at that time – it's now increased to 26 miles.

The vast sweeping curve of Cardigan Bay on the west coast of Wales has comparatively few major lights along its length, although it did have a lightship stationed there in the 1890s. The northern end of the bay is marked by the Lleyn Peninsula and two miles off its southern tip lies Bardsey Island or Ynys Enlli – 'island of the tides'. Bardsey Sound is a well-known navigational danger area as the tides that funnel through it from opposite directions create boiling seas and tidal rips that are exacerbated when wind and tide oppose one another.

About 1½ miles in length and ½ mile across

it's surrounded by jagged outlying rocks. It is an unusual island because at the northern end is a huge hill called Mynydd Enlli which rises to 543ft, while the south of the island is almost flat and used for agriculture by the small but permanent population.

Bardsey has been a place of pilgrimage since the early years of Christianity, but there are signs of settlements on the island that date from earlier periods. The well-known reference to the island as the burial place of twenty thousand saints dates from the early Middle Ages, when three pilgrimages to Bardsey were said to equal one

to Rome. Legends also have it that Bardsey was the last resting place of King Arthur and Merlin the magician – presumably along with their final resting places in Somerset and Cornwall!

It was an obvious candidate for a lighthouse, and a suggestion from William Morris in 1801 started the ball rolling. Joseph Nelson is officially credited as being the designer and builder of the 99ft tower and keepers' accommodation, although it has all the characteristics of a tower designed by Daniel Alexander who succeeded Samuel Wyatt as the Trinity House architect. It was built between 1820–21 at a place called Pen Diban. The tower cost £5,470 12s 6d and the lantern a further £2,950 16s 7d. The first lighthouse keeper was a James Vanston from Devon. A foghorn was added in 1878 which meant the lightship in Cardigan Bay could be withdrawn.

What makes this such an unusual and note-worthy lighthouse is the fact that the tower is square. It, and Coquet (see earlier entry), are the only square towers that Trinity House maintain. When first built it was completely white but has now been painted with red and white horizontal bands to improve its visibility as a daymark.

The lighthouse was supplied by a tender from Aberdaron whose first master, Thomas Williams, was an islander. While returning to Bardsey on 30th November 1822 – only a year after the lighthouse had been lit – the tender struck a rock off the island and Thomas Williams together with his 20-year-old daughter Sydney and four others lost their lives. They are buried in the churchyard at Aberdaron. Thomas Williams was succeeded

THE LIGHTHOUSE FROM EAST, BARDSEY ISLAND.

Copyright. Bd. I.77.

BARDSEY FROM THE SOUTH A./29302

Above: From the air we can see that Bardsey Island has a large hill – Mynydd Enlli – at one end and a low flat area where the lighthouse was built, at the other. The two are connected by a narrow isthmus of land. It's also clear that a large proportion of Bardsey is under cultivation by its permanent population.

Left: There's quite an extensive cluster of buildings within the lighthouse compound. The keepers' cottages attached to the tower have a particularly attractive design that sets them apart from the usual, functional appearance of a lighthouse cottage.

as master of the tender by another islander, John Williams, who became 'King' of Bardsey but was himself drowned in 1841.

Electricity was brought to the lighthouse in 1965 and the keepers were taken away in 1987. In August 2009 Trinity House proposed some significant changes at Bardsey. The traditional rotating lens and lantern would be replaced by an LED lantern which would give a considerable reduction in maintenance. Its light character would change from five white flashes every 15 seconds to one red flash every five seconds with

a corresponding reduction in range from 26 to 18 miles. The fog signal would also be discontinued. It's a good illustration of how lighthouse authorities, right from their earliest days have always kept abreast of, and implemented, the very latest navigational technology. LED lanterns are just the latest innovation that follow-on from radar beacons, wind and solar power generation, and AIS (Automatic Identification System). They might not look as nice as the rotating rings of glass prisms, but they will probably be just as reliable.

Position:	Cardigan Bay, 2½ mls SW of Lleyn Peninsula, Gwynedd
Constructed:	1821
Designer:	Joseph Nelson
Builder:	Joseph Nelson
Tower height:	99ft (30m)
Light character:	W Gp Fl (5) ev 15 secs
Range:	26 mls
Fog warning:	Nautophone (2) ev 45 secs
Automated:	1987

ST TUDWAL'S

Just around the corner from Bardsey is another significant island lighthouse situated on the small island of St Tudwal's Island West, (there is actually a St Tudwal's Island East as well) close to Abersoch on the south side of the Lleyn Peninsula. Its construction was suggested because the light from Bardsey lighthouse was obscured by the hill of Mynydd Enlli from certain directions on the west side of Tremadog Bay. This was a particular problem for vessels carrying general cargo and slate into and out of ports such as Porthmadog.

Trinity House purchased St Tudwal's West Island in 1876 for the sum of £111, and the construction of a 36ft tower and keepers' dwellings was completed the following year to a design by James Nicholas Douglass – who had yet to build his masterpiece on the Eddystone. The tower has one of Douglass's famous helically-framed lanterns that subsequently became commonplace at Trinity House lights. It straddles the summit ridge on the island and everything is enclosed within a sturdy, but perfectly square, boundary wall.

But the real significance of this lighthouse is that in 1922 the lighthouse was converted to automatic operation with the light being switched on and off by a sun valve. It meant that following the introduction of the equipment the lighthouse could be demanned and the keepers withdrawn. This made St Tudwal's one of the earliest Trinity House automatic lighthouses – a full half century before the cost-effective benefits of automation became widespread. The dwellings next to the tower were subsequently sold in 1935. There was a further modernisation and conversion to solar power in 1995.

Position:	Cardigan Bay, 2 mls SE of Abersoch, Lleyn Peninsula, Gwynedd
Constructed:	1876-77
Designer:	James Nicholas Douglass
Builder:	James Nicholas Douglass
Tower height:	36ft (11m)
Light character:	W+R Fl ev 15 secs
Range:	W14, R10 mls
Fog warning:	None
Automated:	1922

ST. TUDWALL'S LIGHTHOUSE. ABERSOCH. PWLLHELI.

Left: With no permanent population, this large gathering at St Tudwal's lighthouse is either the keepers and their families, or visitors. The three to the left of the gateposts, and the one on the extreme right are certainly keepers wearing their Trinity House hats. As to the remaining mix of men, women and children, including the six on the lantern gallery – it's anyone's guess.

Below: A nice aerial shot of St Tudwal's West showing the lighthouse in its square compound on the summit of the island.

S.ᵗ Tudwals Island, West

SOUTH BISHOP

Five miles south west of St David's Head in Pembrokeshire, straddling the point at which vessels from Liverpool and the Irish Sea would make their turn for the Bristol Channel or South Wales ports is a cluster of about 20 rocks and reefs known collectively as The Bishops and Clerks. Some of them are sizeable lumps rising sheer from the sea, others are barely visible at low tide.

They claimed many vessels, and as sea trade increased in the 19th century there was much concern from traders using the ports of Cardigan and Bristol in particular. Trinity House was petitioned in both 1831 and 1834 for a lighthouse on these rocks, but it was another four years before work was started on a lighthouse designed by James Walker.

The obvious candidate for the site of the beacon was the southernmost rock of the group known as the South Bishop (to differentiate it from the North Bishop at the opposite end). It rose sharply 100ft out of the sea, and was almost vertical on most of its faces, but there was room on its summit for a 36ft brick tower and lantern which was eventually lit in 1839. It even had a keepers' house attached, which was allegedly for the use of two families, although it's doubtful if any families actually lived in such an exposed dwelling.

The south-western face of South Bishop slopes

a little more than the others – sufficient to direct the full force of a south-westerly gale up the rock, flooding the courtyard and breaking windows. The first helipad was constructed in 1971 at the bottom of this ramp and its use was therefore constrained by the state of wind and tide. It was abandoned after some years for a drier pad on the summit.

As well as being in the middle of a busy coastal shipping lane, South Bishop lighthouse was also built in the path of migrating birds. The brilliance of its light often drew them into its rays only to dash themselves against the lantern windows. So many were killed that Trinity House, together with the RSPB, built special bird perches on the lantern for use during the migrating season, considerably reducing the mortality rate.

The paraffin lamps were removed in 1959 in favour of electricity, and automatic equipment arrived in 1983. Its lantern is now the oldest original working lighthouse lantern in Wales.

South Bishop's Lighthouse, off St. David's Head.   Fred. J. Jones

Above: Taken from a passing boat, this card was posted in 1909. We can see the flights of steps with a white handrail leading down to one of the landing stages. On the summit the tower is connected to a large two-storey keepers' house, and if we look carefully there's a keeper on the lantern gallery and a line of washing drying in the yard.

Position:	St George's Channel, 5 mls SW of St David's Head, Pembrokeshire
Constructed:	1839
Designer:	James Walker
Builder:	James Walker
Tower height:	36ft (11m)
Light character:	W Fl ev 5 secs
Range:	19 mls
Fog warning:	Horn (3) ev 45 secs
Automated:	January 1984

The South Bishop Lighthouse.

Left: This is a view from the other side of the island and shows the main relief landing. In fact, the Trinity House flag on the flagpole means it is probably relief day at the South Bishop. This rare sepia card dates from 1927 and shows that since the previous card was photographed, a substantial foghorn house has appeared on the opposite side of the tower to the keepers' house – which is not present in the card above.

SKOKHOLM ISLAND

Skokholm is the last in a triangle of Pembrokeshire lighthouses (together with the Smalls and South Bishop) that have kept ships clear of the rocks, reefs and cliffs of this particularly treacherous stretch of coastline, and guided them safely into Milford Haven or up the Bristol Channel.

The island of Skokholm is named after the old Norse words for *'wooded island'* – although there aren't many trees there now – is just 1¼ miles long by ½ mile wide, and lies south of St Brides Bay, about 4½ miles north-east of the light on St Ann's Head. It's also a 240-acre nature reserve and a SSSI (Site of Special Scientific Interest) specifically because of its wildlife and geology and is therefore designated as National Nature Reserve.

The lighthouse sits on top of jagged 100ft sandstone cliffs at the south-west corner of the island near Quarry Point. It's a comparatively new Trinity House light – it wasn't started until World War I and a plaque inside the tower records that it was officially opened in 1915, although records suggest that it wasn't actually lit until 1916.

Sir Thomas Matthews built a square keepers' accommodation block, on top of which he put an elegant hexagonal brick tower and lantern 56ft high. It is thought to be the last British lighthouse built from stone, but all traces of the masonry are now lost under a coat of render.

Before the lighthouse could be built on the island, a jetty had to be constructed at South Haven to land building materials safely. After the station had been completed, this jetty was used for landing stores and supplies, which were then carried the mile to the lighthouse on two small trucks running on a narrow gauge railway.

The trucks were originally pulled by a donkey which somehow always seemed to know when a relief day was due because he would deliberately hide – often standing motionless under an overhanging rock. The colour of the rock blended perfectly with the donkey's grey coat. The keepers often walked miles combing the island for him. On all other days the donkey would come when called. The pony that replaced him apparently soon learnt similar tricks because he did his best to cause spillages every time he had to pull the trucks, scattering coal and stores all over the place. A more reliable tractor was subsequently used. This story, while entertaining, is also remarkable for its similarity to the one of the donkey at Pentland Skerries (see earlier entry). Lighthouse donkeys must have a cussedness gene bred into them!

The lighthouse was automated in December 1983 and is now powered by solar energy. Its single flash every 10 seconds is both red and white depending on the direction it is viewed from. It has a unique red filter modification on the landward side to prevent birds being dazzled at night and flying into the lantern. Although keepers no longer live at the station, Skokholm Island is still inhabited as the island has been designated as Britain's oldest bird sanctuary with ornithologists from all over the world visiting the specially-built hide to study the rare and unusual bird life.

Position:	St George's Channel, 4 mls NW of St Ann's Head, Pembrokeshire
Constructed:	1915–16
Designer:	Thomas Matthews
Builder:	Thomas Matthews
Tower height:	58ft (18m)
Light character:	W+R Fl ev 10 secs
Range:	15 mls
Fog warning:	Discontinued 1983
Automated:	December 1983

Above: It looks as though there is some kind of refurbishment or repainting going on at Skokholm in this card. The building is certainly not looking at its best – the paint has been stripped back to the render and repairs have been made, before a fresh white coat can be applied. The Trinity House flag suggests that it could be a relief day. The tramway that connects the light with the landing stage at the other end of the island is obvious, but the donkey that pulled the trucks along it is not!

LUNDY ISLAND

Rising 400 feet out of the sea where the Bristol Channel meets the Atlantic Ocean is the island of Lundy (Norse: *Puffin island*), a granite plateau 3½ miles long by ¾ mile wide. Reefs and rocks surround its 20 miles of rugged coastline and make an approach to the island difficult for the unknowing sailor. Vast numbers of vessels have been wrecked around its ferocious granite cliffs, particularly on the exposed west and south coasts.

As early as 1786 a lighthouse was proposed on the summit of the island at Beacon Hill by a consortium of Bristol merchants, although nothing actually appeared for another 33 years when, in 1819, Trinity House themselves proposed the erection of a lighthouse. The builder was Joseph Nelson, and the architect was Daniel Alexander, whose previous work included another famous granite structure – Dartmoor prison! Between them they produced an elegant granite tower 96ft high with the keepers' houses adjoining, that cost £10,276 19s 11d.

An innovation in lighthouse optics was used here for the first time; two lights were shown from the tower, the lower was a fixed white light; the upper was a white quick-flashing light, every 60 seconds. However, there was a problem; the upper light revolved so quickly that no period of darkness was detectable between the flashes so in effect this also appeared as a fixed light. They were shown from elevations of 508ft and 538ft respectively and from five miles away the two lights merged into one.

It was this appearance of being a fixed light that contributed to a disaster in November 1828. The ship *La Jeune Emma* en route from Martinique to Cherbourg arrived in Carmarthen Bay in thick fog, mistook the Lundy lights for the fixed light of Ushant in France and went onto the rocks. Of the 19 people on board 13 were lost including a niece of the Empress Josephine.

LANDING BEACH, LUNDY AND SOUTH LIGHTHOUSE

Above: Lundy South sits on an area of level ground blasted out of the rocks above the landing beach and accessed by endless flights of steps.

The card carries one of the Lundy Puffin stamps that have been issued since 1929 as a way of offsetting the cost of handling the mail on Lundy after the Post Office closed in 1927. They have been used ever since featuring a vast array of subjects, denominations and colours – both definitives and commemoratives. The One Puffin red on this card was issued in 1957. At one time there was even a Half Puffin stamp, although goodness knows what they did in the island shop if you didn't have the right money and needed a Half Puffin in change!

LUNDY SOUTH	
Position:	Bristol Channel, SE corner of Lundy Island.
Constructed:	1896–97
Designer:	Daniel Alexander
Builder:	Joseph Nelson
Tower height:	52ft (16m)
Light character:	W Fl ev 5 secs
Range:	15 mls
Fog warning:	Horn (1) ev 25 secs
Automated:	December 1994

OLD LIGHTHOUSE, LUNDY AND FAMOUS LUNDY PONIES

Left: This was the original lighthouse at Beacon Hill. The keepers' house and tower were both built from Lundy granite. The two Lundy ponies are part of a herd established in 1929 capable of surviving a harsh climate and poor grazing on the cliff-top plateau. They are a very hardy type of pony – if they were required on the mainland, they could be made to swim over, towed behind a boat!

Below: A very accurately-dated card showing Lundy South light when it was less than ten years old, and just a few of the flights of steps the keepers had to climb to get to it.

This wasn't its only problem. At an elevation of 540ft above high water it was the highest in Britain at that time. The installation of a new optic in 1857 still didn't prevent the light being shrouded in fog at certain times and rendering it useless as a navigation aid. So many ships ploughed onto the rocks around Lundy when the fog was down that Trinity House was constantly receiving complaints about the light. They were virtually forced into making plans to construct new lighthouses at lower elevations at the extremities of the island.

The old lighthouse was abandoned in 1897 and two new lighthouses were built on the North and South ends of the island by Sir Thomas Matthews. Lundy South required an area of rock to be blasted and levelled before its 52ft tower, which stood 175ft above high water, could be built. These excavations meant that the light was visible for 20 miles from all directions and now reached the North Devon coast. Most of the equipment inside the old light was moved to Lundy South.

Lundy North has a 56ft tower and sits on a ledge 156ft above high water with a light that was visible for 19 miles in good weather. A short distance from the tower an aerial ropeway was constructed for unloading supplies from the lighthouse tender. Once they were winched onto the island they were delivered the final 100 yards to the lighthouse on a small tramway.

Both stations were wisely equipped with fog signals – Lundy North had a siren, and Lundy South, to differentiate it, had an explosive gun cotton signal fired every 10 minutes. More recently the domed lantern roof you see in these cards at the South light was removed and replaced with a foghorn mounted in a cylindrical tower which formed the new lantern roof.

Lundy Island. The Lighthouse.   13/3/06. Lundy South.

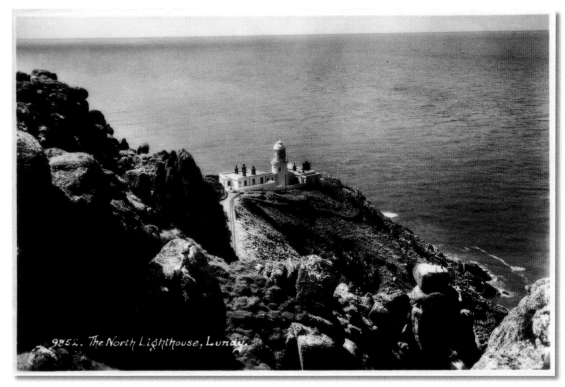

9852. The North Lighthouse, Lundy.

Lundy North had electricity installed in 1971, was automated in 1985 and modernised in 1991 when it was converted to solar power with a new lantern installed on top of the disused fog signal building. The original lantern is now redundant. Lundy South followed with solarisation and automation in December 1994 before the last lighthouse keepers left Lundy for good. The old light has had much renovation and repair by the Landmark Trust who manage the island on behalf of the National Trust and is now a unique holiday let.

LUNDY NORTH

Position:	Bristol Channel, northernmost point of Lundy Island
Constructed:	1896-97
Designer:	Daniel Alexander
Builder:	Joseph Nelson
Tower height:	56ft (17m)
Light character:	W Fl ev 15 secs
Range:	17 mls
Fog warning:	Discontinued 1988
Automated:	1971

Above: A lovely sepia study of Lundy North on its ledge halfway down the cliffs. Leading away from the rear of the buildings we can see the short tramway that delivered stores from the top of the aerial ropeway to the light.

Right: The three keepers of Lundy North in this rare card are actually standing on the tramway. Someone has written the location of the light on the right-hand side, and just above this the two giant foghorn trumpets project from the roof of the foghorn room. Compare this view with the previous card, from a later date, where the foghorn emitters have been modified.

FLATHOLM

The island of Flat Holm breaks out of the Bristol Channel almost midway between Barry and Weston-super-Mare, into the centre of the River Severn estuary. It is a particular hazard for vessels making for Newport, Portishead, Avonmouth and Bristol – even more so when these ports enjoyed much greater trade than now. The need for a lighthouse on the island had been discussed for many years by leading shipmasters and by members of the Society of Merchant Venturers of Bristol but a petition of 1733 and a scheme of 1735 both came to nothing.

At the end of 1736 60 soldiers were drowned when a vessel was wrecked near Flat Holm, which gave greater impetus for further negotiations to erect a light. On 9th April 1737 a William Crispe, supported by the Merchant Venturers was finally granted a patent for a lighthouse from Trinity House together with a lease for 97 years to collect dues. The lease was finally signed and a coal-burning light was first shown on 1st December 1737 from the top of a 67ft circular tower.

Owing to the increased cost of building the structure William Crispe took on a partner, Benjamin Lund, but even their joint funds were insufficient and they were soon bankrupt. To settle their debts they surrendered their lease to Caleb Dickenson, who then became the manager, light dues collector, and keeper of accounts for the Flatholm light.

On the night of 22nd December 1790, a gale of exceptional violence occurred which caused considerable destruction in south-west England and Flatholm lighthouse suffered some damage. The tenant keepers reported that, 'We expected every moment to be our last. At three o'clock on the morning of the 23rd the tower was struck by lightning. The man attending the fire was knocked

THE LIGHTHOUSE, FLAT HOLM.

down and narrowly escaped falling through the stairway. The iron fire grate was smashed to pieces and the top of the tower considerably damaged'. Until repairs were effected a fire was maintained on the headland in front of the lighthouse. Bristol traders however continually complained about the inadequacy of the light and it appears that the owners enjoyed a large income from it but refused to spend an additional £100 or so a year to make it a reasonable aid to shipping.

On 17th November, 1819, Trinity House signed an agreement with William Dickenson – now the principal leaseholder of the lighthouse – to alter

and maintain the light for an annual payment of £400 for the remainder of the lease, at which point the lessees would surrender the property and all light dues to them. The Corporation's surveyor prepared plans for the alterations that involved the massive circular stone tower being increased in height from 68ft to 88ft in order to make a suitable base for the lantern in which they planned to install Argand lamps. The new light was first exhibited on 7th September 1820 as a fixed white light.

In July 1822 an Act was passed by George IV which empowered Trinity House to purchase

Flat Holmes. 104. Weston-S-Mare.

Position:	Bristol Channel, 6 mls S of Cardiff, South Wales
Constructed:	1737, 1819–20
Designer:	William Crispe, William Dickenson
Builder:	William Crispe, William Dickenson
Tower height:	72ft (22m), 99ft (30m)
Light character:	Coal fire, W+R Fl ev 10 secs
Range:	Unknown, W15, R12 mls
Fog warning:	Discontinued
Automated:	January 1988

Previous page: A 1927 sepia card in which we are looking south on Flat Holm towards the lighthouse. On the horizon is the rounded hump of Steep Holm. The two islands are only about 4 miles apart, but Steep Holm is administered by North Somerset and Flat Holm from Cardiff.

Left: Although the island is called Flat Holm (or incorrectly in this card 'Flat Holmes') Trinity House has always called its lighthouse 'Flatholm' – without a space. It is not perfectly flat – but it is flatter than its neighbour Steep Holm. This is a view of Lighthouse Point from the Bristol Channel.

outright the leases of any coastal lights around England and Wales still in private hands, and Flatholm was one they decided to acquire. The value of the remaining 12 years of the lease was estimated at £15,838 10s which was paid to William Dickenson and his executors. Trinity House took possession of the light on 21st March 1823.

In 1825 they made further improvements – raising the lantern another 5ft and installing a fountain oil lamp – followed in 1867 by a new lantern 13ft in diameter that remained until 1969. In 1881 the light was converted to occulting (a method of making the light appear to flash by blocking the light from it by a panel with a clockwork-operated mechanism). Subsequent improvements were made to the burners in the lantern and by 1908 a powerful compressed air fog signal with two horns was installed in a building separate from the lighthouse.

The island is also home to quite a varied array of other buildings and structures. It's littered with redundant military leftovers such as a WWII radar station at its centre together with a cholera isolation hospital. There are remnants of an even greater age dating back several centuries, such as eighteenth century cannon, earthwork emplacements and a defensive ditch which bisects the island – all left as a result of Prime Minister Palmerston's fear that Napoleon III would actually invade!

In February 1902 Flatholm light was the scene of a remarkable phenomenon. During the night a shower of mud fell on the island and the glazing of the lighthouse was covered with a dirty white coating which stuck to the glass like glue and could only be removed with great difficulty. A quantity of fine dust, believed by meteorologists to have been carried in the atmosphere from the Sahara Desert, fell on an area of about 2,000 square miles of south

west England. The mud that covered the lighthouse lantern was some of the dust converted into slime by rain clouds.

Flatholm lighthouse was converted to a rock station in 1929. This meant that the keepers' families who used to live on the island in two cottages adjacent to the tower were now moved into housing ashore. At the same time an additional keeper was appointed, increasing their number to four and enabling the men to serve three months on duty followed by one month ashore. In more recent years, the lighthouse was manned by two sets of three keepers each working one month on the lighthouse followed by one month ashore.

The lighthouse was automated in 1988 and the keepers were withdrawn. In 1997 it was modernised and converted to solar power. Its single white or red flash (depending on where it is viewed from) can be seen for either 15 or 12 miles away.

GODREVY

Left: A very attractive hand-tinted card showing the fine architectural detail of Godrevy's octagonal tower in about 1890. The lantern is glazed in the characteristic James Walker style of tapering glass panes also seen at the Smalls and Needles lighthouses. Four figures are posing outside the gate of the lighthouse, three of whom we presume are the keepers.

Virginia Woolf is alleged to have taken inspiration for her novel *To The Lighthouse* from Godrevy Island light, remembered from her childhood visits to Cornwall and St. Ives in particular. It is situated 3½ miles away across St. Ives Bay, yet only about 200 yards from the nearest point on the mainland to the east of it, but still exposed to the full force of westerly gales.

The coast here is jagged and unforgiving, although not as unforgiving as a dangerous reef called The Stones that extends south-westward towards St. Ives. It has been the final resting place for countless vessels over the centuries, including the *Garland*, which on 30th January 1649 struck Godrevy island in a severe gale. It was apparently carrying many personal effects of Charles I's son – including, it is said, his entire wardrobe! Out of 60 passengers and crew only one man, a small boy and an Irish wolfhound survived.

Between 1820–40 it was estimated that 150 lives were lost because of the lack of a lighthouse to mark Godrevy island and The Stones reef. The wreck that produced the greatest clamour for a light occurred on 30th November 1854, after the 700-ton iron screw steamer *Nile* was totally wrecked on the Outer Stones rocks with the loss of all 60 passengers and crew.

Within two months Trinity House received eight petitions containing 280 signatures of ship owners and merchants. One charitable shipbuilder even offered to provide a light vessel at his own expense to prove that it wasn't necessary to build a masonry tower – a floating navigation aid would do. He anchored his ship close to The Stones but during the following winter its anchor chain snapped in a gale and the vessel was wrecked.

The wrecks continued; the *Maria* in 1855, and the *Josephine*, *Desdemona*, *Ernest* and *Mount Charles* in 1856. Finally, in April 1857 Trinity House got

permission to erect a lighthouse designed by James Walker in the popular hexagonal style of the period. Its long-awaited light first shone out from the top of an 84ft tower on 1st March 1859. Two keepers were originally appointed to the lighthouse to maintain the two lights, one a bright flashing white every 10 seconds, and the other fixed red, which marked the Stones Rocks. Their range was 17 and 15 miles respectively. It cost a very reasonable £7,082 15s 7d.

The original optic revolved on rollers on a circular race and was driven by a clockwork motor, which in turn was driven by a large weight running down a cavity in the wall of the tower. The station was also equipped with a 3cwt bell as a fog signal, struck once every five seconds. The lighthouse was altered in 1939, when a new 2nd order fixed catadioptric lens was installed, together with an acetylene burner fitted with a sun valve. It meant that the keepers could be withdrawn and the lighthouse made automatic – another of Trinity House's earliest automatic stations. Finally the lighthouse was modernised in 1995 when it was converted to solar-powered operation.

Above: This is the view of Godrevy lighthouse from Godrevy Point on the mainland about 1930. The tower was built on the slightly more sheltered side of the island, but with a tall enough tower to enable its flash to be visible from all seaward sectors.

Left: A view of Godrevy lighthouse from sea level showing that some of the lantern panes are obscured so that its flash cannot be seen from the mainland. In front of the tower are steps down to a small landing stage, while all the heavy equipment and stores were landed further to the right at the jetty with a crane.

Position:	Atlantic Ocean, 3½ mls NE of St. Ives, Cornwall
Constructed:	1858–59
Designer:	James Walker
Builder:	James Walker
Tower height:	84ft (26m)
Light character:	W+R Fl ev 10 secs
Range:	W 12, R 9 mls
Fog warning:	Discontinued
Automated:	1939

3 RELIEF DAY

Hauling a relief man into the Eddystone Lighthouse

Vaughan, T. Paul's Photo
Copyright.

Above: Is this a genuine photograph or an attempt at a montage of two separate shots? We'll probably never know. An open rowing boat appears to be almost out of the water as its crew struggles to prevent a keeper they have brought to Eddystone being dashed against the base of the tower. Above us two other keepers are furiously winding a windlass in the winch room to lift the keeper out of the confusion of spray and salt water as quickly as possible. The keeper at this point is completely helpless and entirely in the hands of five other men. All he can do is hang on tight.

Changing the keepers at some of our remotest lighthouses could prove every bit as difficult as their construction. Getting men into and out of granite towers that rose straight out of the sea, or on and off remote islands that offered no obvious safe anchorage, tested the bravery and ingenuity of those carrying out the relief and the keepers being relieved. Basically, it was a procedure that was entirely dependent upon the state of wind and tide. Sometimes the sea was kind and all was well, but winter reliefs were often a fight between the determination and courage of those involved and the strength of the sea to resist them. The sea often won and the relief was cancelled, with the resulting frustration for those still aboard and having to try again when conditions would allow.

The postcards in this chapter give a flavour of what a relief day could be like for the keepers at our most isolated lighthouses. And here it must be remembered that some of the photographers will have suffered the same hardships as the keepers and crew in the open boat to record these events. On many occasions reliefs were attempted in what could only be described as marginal conditions but the relieving boatmen were skilled and wily seamen who knew exactly what was possible and what wasn't. The keepers may have got slightly wet, but better that than another week inside a pillar lighthouse!

Right: A sure sign it was relief day at a remote lighthouse was the flying of the Trinity House or NLB ensign. The only other time it might be seen was when a visit from the Elder Brethren or Commissioners of Northern Lighthouses was expected. But a relief day was far more important to the keepers, and flying the flag was a sign that a visit was expected and everything was ready. Often, as the relief boat approached the keepers gathered on the lantern gallery or at the base of the tower waiting to greet the new keepers and boat crew.

Not all three keepers were changed at once so for the ones staying on board on a relief day it also brought welcome supplies of fresh fruit or vegetables and even out-of-date newspapers and magazines.

This card, posted in 1955, clearly shows the Trinity House flag flying, and two of the three keepers watching the approaching boat anxiously from the gallery. Radiating away from the door of the tower are a series of steps leading to three different landing stages that could be used depending on wind direction and state of the tide. Sometimes conditions might be impossible at all three stages, particularly in winter, and that meant disappointment all round and an extended turn of duty for the keeper(s) who had already done one or two months in the cramped confines of Longships lighthouse.

LANDS END, LONGSHIPS LIGHTHOUSE.

62994

LONGSHIPS LIGHTHOUSE AND RELIEF BOAT, LAND'S END.   119.

Left: The actual exchange of keepers and supplies was done from an open boat rowed from the Trinity House or NLB supply vessel which anchored at a safe distance. This view shows one of the Trinity House tenders taking the short-cut between Lands End and the reef having probably just completed the relief of the Longships light behind. It's heading for Penzance or even possibly for Wolf Rock lighthouse, 8 miles away, to carry out the relief there.

Although difficult to identify, the vessel on this card was one of a fleet of nine that Trinity House had around the time of World War II. They carried names such as *Alert, Arial, Argos, Patricia, Strathearn, Vestal* or *Vigilant* but many of these were lost during the War. These were subsequently replaced by *Winston Churchill, Stella, Siren, Satellite, Mermaid* and a new *Patricia*. Today, the fleet is much reduced to a mere three – *Galatea*, a 'Rapid Intervention Vessel' named *Alert*, and an even newer *Patricia*.

Right: A scene at the Eddystone showing all the clues that it's relief day. What appears to be the Union Jack is flying from the flagpole (although this could be a bit of artistic licence from the person who hand-tinted the card), two keepers are waiting on the set-off which has had a rope erected around it for safety purposes. An open boat is being rowed towards the lighthouse, and in the gap between Smeaton's tower and the present Douglass tower we can see a Trinity House vessel at anchor. The sea looks calm enough to suggest they are going to attempt a relief by tying up at the base of the metal dog steps that lead from the set-off to water level. It's interesting to see that the two giant 40-cwt fog bells are still in evidence hanging from the lantern gallery. They were removed in 1891 which means that this scene can be dated at somewhere between 1882 and 1891.

20148   Plymouth. Eddystone Lighthouse.

The Bell Rock Lighthouse, Arbroath.

Left: In Scotland relief day at an NLB light looked remarkably similar to one at a light around the coasts of England and Wales. This is a hand-tinted card of Bell Rock lighthouse, 12 miles south-east of Arbroath. The NLB flag is flying high while down on the cast iron walkways that provided a level pathway to one of several points where a boat could tie up are two keepers. Behind them are piles of boxes, barrels or sacks that have probably just been delivered and are waiting to be hauled into the tower through the door. There could even be another person climbing the ladder to the door.

Note that the lantern in this view has square panes of glass. Compare these with the view of Bell Rock in Chapter 1 – which are triangular. The change occurred in 1902 when the whole lantern was removed and modernised. Right up to the time of its automation in October 1988 all the reliefs of Bell Rock lighthouse used these metal walkways, the only difference was that in later years instead of a boat mooring next to them, a helicopter landed on them.

Right: Some pillar lights such as Wolf Rock and Beachy Head had huge landing stages built at the bases of their towers so that reliefs could be accomplished with slightly more ease – although I'm sure there are many former Wolf Rock keepers who might disagree with that statement! The problem at Wolf Rock was that the low profile of the rock itself – which was completely covered at high tide – meant there was nowhere a boat could tie up to. The massive masonry landing stage with an iron crane derrick on the end meant keepers and stores could be plucked out of, and dropped into, a waiting boat – providing the sea was calm enough. Often it wasn't and missed reliefs were a frequent event at the Wolf.

In this delightfully-coloured card though, the sea is like a millpond, the relief boat has anchored a few yards off the landing stage and the derrick crane has been rigged and is in use. A very tranquil relief indeed. Compare this with the next card.

The Wolf Rock Lighthouse.

Wolfrock-Leuchtturm an der engl. Küste in Cornwall

auf welchem die Wärter wegen fortwährend schwerer Brandung seit 3 Monaten trotz aller Anstrengungen nicht abgelöst werden konnten.

Left: Unusually, this is a German postcard of an English lighthouse. The Germans too have a fascination with lighthouses and are keen enthusiasts – hence this sepia card of a lighthouse hundreds of miles from their own coastline. As you can see it's a very different day at Wolf Rock to the previous card. There is a flag flying and a very forlorn silhouette of a keeper on the gallery who knows that there will be absolutely no chance of a relief today, even though the boat has got this close.

The German caption on this card reads, 'Wolf Rock lighthouse on the English coast in Cornwall, on which the keepers – because of heavy surf for three months, despite all efforts could not be changed'.

Right: This is how men and stores were transferred from boat to lighthouse at several of the pillar lights around the Cornish coast, but this relief is at one of the landings of the Longships lighthouse. It shows a keeper being hoisted into the air by the derrick crane – the main mast of which was permanently embedded into the landing. They used a windlass which needed four men to operate it.

This keeper looks like he's arriving for his turn of duty, but the trickier operation was to get the keepers going ashore into the boat unscathed – and dry! They were attached to the rope, hoisted into the air and swung out over the boat, which would still be rising and falling with the swell. With careful judgement and skill from those on the windlass and in the boat the precious cargo could be lowered into the boat as it rose to meet it, and all would be well. But this could be a difficult and dangerous manoeuvre at some lighthouses where the boat was anchored a few yards off the landing, resulting in stores or keepers being dumped in the sea before being hurriedly hauled out again. A dunking in the sea was usually referred to as a 'wet' relief and there will have been few keepers of this era who did not experience such an uncomfortable transfer!

RELIEF DAY. BISHOP LIGHTHOUSE. No 100.

Left: Bishop Rock, Eddystone, Longships and Wolf Rock were the notorious Trinity House stations for wet reliefs or missed reliefs altogether. Things didn't improve until they all had helipads erected over their lanterns in the 1970s and '80s and the state of the sea became irrelevant to the relief. Only fog would cause a postponement.

This spectacular view from the lantern gallery of Bishop Rock shows the kind of distances involved between the tower and waiting boat. We can see that the two-man windlass here is actually on the narrow set-off, and the rope rises from it, around a pulley on the lantern gallery, and then falls into the boat. At an appropriate point on the rope a bowline is tied (a non-slipping knot which forms a loop) into which the keeper can put a foot while he hangs on to the rope with both hands for dear life. As the windlass is cranked he is lifted up from the set-off and then starts an immediate descent. The critical manoeuvre here is for the men in the boat to pull the weight of the rope and its human cargo away from the tower and into the boat as it lowered – quite some feat for the team in the boat that is bobbing like a cork. Any misjudgement or slackening of the rope caused by the boat rising on a big wave could find the unfortunate keeper dunked in the boiling waters or crashing into the tower before he reached the safety of his transport ashore.

In this card the cargo looks non-human and is probably stores, drinking water or coal for the lighthouse.

Right: This is what the operation looks like from the boat. The keeper on the rope has one foot in a loop and his other leg draped over the rope. The two men on the windlass are lowering him smoothly into the boat which is held roughly in position by the rope on the background looped over a metal stanchion driven into the rock, and a stern anchor. It's over 40 feet from sea level to the set-off at this point, depending on the state of the tide, but such was the skill of all those involved a dunking in the sea was the exception rather than the rule.

BISHOP LIGHTHOUSE RELIEF, SCILLY. No.149.

Left: Nearly there! Only a few more feet to go before this keeper is safely in the boat. Note that he's clutching the rope with bare hands and is wearing his Trinity House cap and greatcoat for the occasion – but no life jacket. In fact, there are not many life jackets in evidence in any of the cards in this chapter – and one wonders what the reaction of these long-serving, sea-weathered men might have been if it were suggested that they had to put on a life jacket, or a wet suit, or a high visibility 'bib' for their 10-second trip on the end of a rope!

Right: From another angle the sheer size of the base of the tower becomes apparent. This keeper is leaving with what could be a painting he has done, all carefully wrapped in brown paper, in the crook of his arm. Many keepers at rock lighthouses had hobbies which they could indulge while on duty. Reading and painting were obvious ones and many keepers became extraordinarily well read and could converse about most matters with some insight. Some were keen fishermen and had developed a method of 'kite fishing' from the set-offs, while matchstick models and ships in bottles were other favourites. As television, radio and the telephone became commonplace, a lot of these traditional hobbies died out.

Left: The ritual of the changing of the keepers at Bishop Rock lighthouse became a popular tourist attraction of the Scilly Isles with small flotillas of boats setting out from St Mary's on appropriate days to witness the drama. Several boats full of holidaymakers are watching a relief on a fine summer's day during the 1960s in this colour view. It all came to an end in August 1976 when the first helicopter relief of keepers took place on the newly-installed helideck.

It's not quite low water in this card, but I have seen other photographs that show 18 steps carved into the rock from the base of the tower down to water level. If conditions were calm enough, it was possible to step off a boat onto the rock, but then it was a strenuous climb up 45 vertical metal dog-steps just to reach the entrance door, before all the interior steps were negotiated.

Right: If Bishop Rock or Wolf Rock were the nightmare postings for Trinity House keepers then Dubh Artach was the NLB's equivalent. The humped nature of the rock and the fierce tidal surges around it meant that the sea was seldom calm around Dubh Artach, and in winter it could be positively evil with overdue reliefs extending into weeks.

We can get a good idea of why by studying this card that shows a 1960s relief. There were only two places it was possible to get a boat close enough to the rock for a relief and one of them, on the right-hand side of this card, is being used. A metal walkway has been built projecting out into the sea. On the end is a derrick crane that is in the process of swinging a keeper into an open boat that has disappeared behind the wall of white water. And this is a reasonably good day at Dubh Artach!

The remains of the barrack legs used by the men building the lighthouse can be seen to the left of the tower. These were dismantled when it was decided to build a helipad on the rock in the 1970s to help with its automation.

DHUHEARTACH LIGHTHOUSE, ARGYLL.

EDDYSTONE LIGHTHOUSE, PLYMOUTH.

6

Left: The end of a successful relief at the Eddystone in calm conditions. There are six men, a mixture of keepers and Trinity House boat crew, rowing an open boat away from the lighthouse towards another boat that we can't see. Already the new keepers have moved their gear and supplies inside the tower and the ropes used to lift things in and out of the boat are nowhere to be seen. Only the rope 'handrail' that was threaded through rings embedded in the tower wall remains.

Right: The Needles lighthouse actually had a landing stage at which a small relief boat could tie up and unload in comparative safety. This is a modern painting done by Peter Leath and published by the Isle of Wight Postcard Club as a Limited Edition postcard. It shows a scene from about 1896 of the relief of the present lighthouse. Pilot boat No.6 *Alacrity* has just delivered a Christmas tree and supplies to the keepers who can be seen to the left of the tower on the landing stage. This was a tradition that continued right up until 1994 when the last keepers left the lighthouse. When the tower was built it didn't have a red band, and there is even some conjecture that the band was originally black before it became red.

Left: Relief day was also the time that stores were replenished at lighthouses. Everything required at a remote lighthouse for its efficient operation was usually delivered by boat. The fuel for power, light and heat; paint, polish, soap, light bulbs, drinking water etc – the list is endless. This timeless scene is taking place at one of our most well known lighthouses – South Stack. The light sits on the summit of a small island that is in turn close to the edge of a larger island (Anglesey) and connected to it by a suspension bridge.

An unidentified Trinity House vessel stands off while some of its crew help unload a considerable number of wooden barrels which, if we are to believe the caption, contain oil. These have obviously been winched from a smaller boat that has anchored at the base of the cliffs on which the lighthouse sits. The fuel would be used either in the diesel generators that provided the power for the light, or in the earlier oil lamps. It's difficult to tell from this undated card.

Right: St Abb's Head is actually an isolated Northern Lighthouse Board shore station on the east coast of Scotland near Eyemouth. It is approached along a narrow and winding track so most of its stores came by sea and were landed at this jetty, a half-mile or so to the west of the lighthouse.

The caption tells us that it's in Pettycarwick Bay, although modern maps refer to it as Pettico Wick Bay. The boat is carrying almost as many crew as stores. Seven men are in the boat and another one waits on the jetty. We can't identify the actual stores but they look like consumables rather than edible.

Right: This looks like an early colour photo rather than a hand-tinted black and white card. A sheltered creek at the Casquets lighthouse (notice the alternative spelling) is where the relief boat anchored while keepers were changed and stores delivered. We can see that there's an aerial ropeway above the larger white boat that obviously delivered its cargo up to the lighthouse buildings on the summit of the island. The white tower in the top corner is one of the three original towers built here that is now defunct.

RELIEF BOAT
AT CASQUETTES   CONOLLY COPYRIGHT.

RELIEF DAY, ROUND ISLAND, SCILLY . No 742

Left: Round Island rises sheer out of the blue waters of Scilly on all sides so when Trinity House decided to build a lighthouse there in 1886 there was precious little choice for a landing site for men and materials. At its southern tip there are two small outliers – Camber Rocks – and the gap between Round Island and the nearest one was sufficiently sheltered from the roaring Atlantic to allow construction of a landing stage at the bottom of the cliff face. Flights of stone steps were hewn out of the rock from the summit to the waterline, crevices in the cliffs were filled in by stone masons who shaped their stones to fit the natural contours until eventually there was access for boats to unload their cargo and for it to be hauled to the top of the island.

This rare card shows that creek with a relief boat anchored in mid channel by ropes attached to two overhead cables spanning the gap. Even this comparatively small boat tows an even smaller one behind it. But notice how the rock staircases cling to the natural face of the rock and where a flat platform is required this is achieved by filling in the fissures of the cliffs.

This was the way that keepers were changed until the day the helicopters took over. Viewed from this angle it has more than a passing similarity to the landing at the Flannan Isles which has flight after flight of steps leading down into a deep gulley to a landing from which the three keepers were supposedly lost in 1900. We can also see in this view that besides the two cables that hold the boat steady, there is a third dark cable forming an aerial ropeway to pluck items from the boat and deliver them effortlessly to the top of the cliffs.

Right: A closer view of the Round Island landing showing even more clearly how the masons built the platform by filling in around the existing contours of the rocks. Overhead we can see the two ropes that the larger boat from the previous card is attached to, and how the even smaller boat is used to deliver personnel to the bottom of the steps. There are already four men in the tiny rowing boat and it looks like another two keepers with their hand luggage are coming down the steps to join them. The state of the sea is also a lot worse than in the previous view and the tide appears to be racing through the narrow gully. Fortunately it's only a few yards to the other boat, but with a possible six passengers on board (none of whom are wearing life jackets!) it will require a bit a skill and careful seamanship to cover just these few yards across a fierce current.

THE LANDING-PLACE AT THE MUCKLE FLUGGA LIGHTHOUSE, UNST, SHETLAND.

Left: This is the landing at Muckle Flugga lighthouse that was known as the 'comb' – where boat reliefs could only be attempted in near-perfect conditions such as we see in this card. We're looking north towards Out Stack, the northernmost piece of Britain before the Arctic Circle and just visible to the left of the card.

The open boat is secured to a mooring line that stretches across the comb. The lighthouse is actually high up on the left-hand side of this view, but the landing stage with its handrail is on the right. What we can't see is that the path to the light doubles back on itself behind the silhouette of a man and the jagged pinnacle and crosses the water in front of us on a bridge on which the photographer is probably standing. This leads to the bottom of a flight of 246 steps up the lighthouse. Heavy stores were hauled to the summit of the island on a wire rope.

Another rare card showing everyday life at the very edge of Britain.

Right: Just as remote as Muckle Flugga was Sule Skerry. Here's another very early card that you might imagine wouldn't have much of a market. Unloading sacks of coal from an open boat tied up in a creek on an uninhabited island (apart from the keepers) 40 miles from the next nearest landfall isn't something you'd see in postcard racks today. Yet somebody took the trouble to photograph an ordinary everyday scene and publish it as a postcard. Today, it's an important document of social history because we are witnessing exactly how the fuel was delivered to Britain's most exposed lighthouse – in sacks in an open boat that had been despatched from a bigger boat that would be anchored half a mile or so away. They were removed from the smaller boat by crane and placed into a small railway truck. This ran on a tramway from the landing to the lighthouse in the middle of the island. A fascinating little cameo.

LANDING COAL. SULE SKERRY LIGHTHOUSE. N.S.

4 WILD WINDS AND WHITE WATER

Eddystone Lighthouse in Storm

Above: Being regarded as the most famous lighthouse in the world has meant that Eddystone featured extensively on early postcards and you'll see more of them in this chapter. For most people, the image on a postcard would be their only sight of the lighthouse. The caption of this lovely 1904 sepia card 'Eddystone Lighthouse in Storm' shows exactly that, together with a storm-tossed ship on the left – and a flock of birds whose distinctive black wing tips bear more than a passing resemblance to gannets.

Lighthouses are subjected to some of the worse excesses of Nature we can imagine. A wild sea is a powerful and destructive force, and when combined with a tearing gale the combination can wreak havoc and destruction. The very purpose of a lighthouse is to be placed at the forefront of this struggle between Man and Nature – to warn of the dangers on which it stands. Inevitably they experience the full fury of the elements, but thanks to the genius and skill of their engineers, most of our remote lighthouses are still standing unscathed. Bell Rock will have withstood two centuries of wind and waves in 2011, but Bishop Rock and Eddystone have both had towers swept away by an ocean in fury, and beacons on The Smalls, Eddystone and Longships were replaced before they suffered the same fate.

Really wild seas were always popular subjects for postcards because they tried to illustrate what most people not intimately connected with the sea could only imagine. But it was difficult because it was almost impossible to photograph such events first-hand. An open boat pitching wildly in stormy seas was no place for a photographer trying to set up an early wooden camera on a tripod. However, you'll see there are some cards in this chapter that are actual photographs, but more often than not a postcard of a tearing gale with mountainous seas was the product of an artist's imagination, or even a combination of the two.

Right: Artists' impressions of rough seas were far commoner than actual photographs – for obvious reasons. As you examine the cards in this chapter look out for the elements that all the artists seem to imagine are necessary in such a scene. Lots of white water and spray of course, usually breaking on the rocks or climbing up the tower itself, but notice also the flocks of disturbed sea birds flying around or close to the tower. Couple this with dark skies and vessels sailing uncomfortably close to the lighthouse – sometimes on the horizon, sometimes a little closer, but always at a giddy angle – and you have an almost perfect 'lighthouse-in-a-storm' picture. The only other element that's missing from this colourful 1944 card of the Bell Rock is some floating wreckage – a mast or sail from a vessel that has been driven too close in the storm and paid the price. But don't worry, that'll be along in a moment.

BELL ROCK LIGHTHOUSE, INCHCAPE ROCK.

Earbalestier.

Les Casquets.

Left: A big wave swamps the bow of a fairly sizeable but unidentified two-masted vessel causing it to almost broach as it struggles past the Casquets lighthouse off Guernsey. The three original towers have been caught in a shaft of sunlight breaking through the dark skies. In the bottom right-hand corner the card is identified as an 'oilette'. This was a process that gave a textured surface to the card – much like the original oil painting from which it was made.

Right: 'The Chicken Lighthouse' referred to in this card's caption is Chicken Rock lighthouse off the southern tip of the Isle of Man. This is not a particularly accurate representation of the light – more of a 'generic' lighthouse than anything the Stevensons produced. But there's lots of spray and spume as the storm drives waves against the rugged coast of the Calf of Man island. Perhaps the circling seabirds are storm petrels, otherwise known as Mother Carey's Chickens, who used the rock on which the lighthouse stands as a favourite perch and so gave it a fitting name.

THE CHICKEN LIGHTHOUSE, I.O.M.

Longships Lighthouse

Left: A sepia card this time, with more than a passing similarity to the previous one. Only the distressed seabirds are absent. It's a wild night on the Longships in this 1912 card, scudding clouds partly obscure the moon, but the lantern is lit to warn any vessels foolish enough to be out on such a night of the dangers below. The representation of the lighthouse is a fairly accurate drawing of William Douglass' 1873 tower, and the amount of white water driven against the reef by a tearing gale is by no means exaggerated.

Right: Another lovely 'oilette' card where you can actually see some of the texturing of the surface. Eddystone's light is flashing but it doesn't appear to be night. A ketch with a few sails still up is being driven past the reef at quite a speed I would imagine. The stump of Smeaton's tower is clearly visible, so it's a scene representing a time after 1883.

Left: Here's the floating wreckage I promised earlier, and quite a substantial piece it is too. Probably the mast of a vessel that has been driven onto the Eddystone reef, and there's another ship struggling past without sails on the left-hand side. The artist of this work clearly has no idea as to what goes on in a lighthouse lantern and the kind of beam it produces. The light from the illuminant is turned into parallel rays by the circulating prisms of glass and emerges as a powerful beam, parallel with the sea, and never as depicted in this view. A pity, because the appearance of the lighthouse is fairly accurate, and we can even see Smeaton's stump emerging from the waves just to the left of the broken spar whose end has been splintered.

Right: We'll now have a look at some real photographs of lighthouses in wild conditions. The weather on this card is certainly different to the one at Fair Isle South in the previous chapter. We can't see it, but we know that when this shot was taken the wind must have been strong enough to stir all the water in the little inlets around the lighthouse into white foam – but not strong enough to prevent the photographer venturing out. To the right of the lighthouse is the foghorn tower with the horn projecting out of it. This was the last Scottish lighthouse to have keepers. When they finished their final duty in March 1998, in the presence of HRH The Princess Royal, it was the end of 200 years of lighthouse keepers at the Northern Lighthouse Board.

SOUTH LIGHTHOUSE, FAIR ISLE.

PHOTO: J.D.RATTAR

T 108   LUNDY NORTH END LIGHTHOUSE IN A STORM.   PUBLISHED BY
                                                              TWISS BROS., ILFRACOMBE.

Left: Lots of white caps in this view of Lundy North light in a westerly gale. Two giant foghorns project from the roof of a building containing engines that would have produced the compressed air to drive the horns. Behind the tower is the keepers' accommodation.

Right: This view looks down on the 1902 Beachy Head lighthouse from the top of the chalk cliffs. The tide is rushing in, driven by a strong wind to produce white water as far as the eye can see. This card also gives us a good view of the landing stage attached to the lighthouse and used for the relief of keepers. It's a smaller version of the one at Wolf Rock. There are flights of steps down to sea level and the waiting boat, and we can just see the bottom of the derrick crane post embedded in the landing stage.

Rough Seas, Beachy Head Lighthouse, Eastbourne.

Stormy Seas on Skerries Lighthouse
Height of Tower 160 Ft.   Nº5

Left: Now this is a stormy sea, and by the look of it the photographer did very well to remain upright to take the shot. This is not the Skerries lighthouse off the coast of Anglesey as its caption might suggest, but Out Skerries in the Shetlands. The islet is called Bound Skerry and it's a bleak place for a lighthouse. There's nothing on the island except Thomas and David Stevenson's 1858 lighthouse tower – even the keepers' accommodation was on another island. And when winter storms hit they smash into the island and its solitary tower with a fury. The caption should explain that it's the top of the tower that is 160 feet above sea level, but it makes little difference when the waves are clearly reaching that height! The card is dated 1936 but scenes like this could occur several times each winter in Shetland.

Right and below right: Because Longships lighthouse was built on the outermost rock of the reef it's the point of first contact for any waves driven across the Atlantic by a storm. They smash against the stepped base of the tower and explode upwards, sometimes to the height of the lantern or the present helideck. Photographs of the top half of the lighthouse rising out of a jumble of white water are common and made popular postcards – like these two. Because the tower was only a mile away from the mainland they were not particularly difficult pictures to take. All you needed was a sturdy tripod set up on the cliffs at Land's End supporting a camera with a telephoto lens – and a westerly gale driving the swell against the Longships reef. Then it was just a case of sitting and waiting for the waves to strike.

Rough Sea, Longships Lighthouse, Land's End   PN1236

WOLF ROCK LIGHTHOUSE

Left: This photograph of Wolf Rock was definitely taken from a boat, and it must have been a very uncomfortable journey to get there. It's difficult to tell but the waves seem to be breaking against the stone landing stage rather than the tower itself. Nevertheless, it would still be very uncomfortable in the lighthouse. Many keepers stationed here report how the tower used to shudder when struck by a large wave, and as the water climbed upward past the windows of the bedrooms or kitchen it would go dark for a few seconds before the water fell away. There are some spectacular photographs of Wolf Rock, taken from an aircraft, with just the lantern sticking out of a column of white water. It was such photographs that probably influenced Trinity House's decision to make Wolf Rock the first British lighthouse to be fitted with a helideck in 1973. No more missed reliefs for its grateful keepers.

Right: Dubh Artach rises out of the waves at the head of a submarine trench that stretches away from it for 80 miles into the wild Atlantic. David and Thomas Stevenson, the lighthouse's engineers remarked that this 'funnel-shaped deep track, receiving directly the seas and currents of the Atlantic Ocean, must have some effect in concentrating the waves on the lighthouse rock at the head of this submerged valley, and may therefore account for the seemingly abnormal seas to which the tower is subjected ...'

This card shows us what some of those 'abnormal seas' look like on a comparatively placid day at Dubh Artach. There's white water breaking on all sides of the rock and running off it along the cracks and fissures of its surface. There's even a brave party of men on the right-hand side in an open boat. It looks remarkably like a relief is being attempted, but as there is no flag flying and no derrick crane rigged to enable the transfer of men, it could be that conditions are severe enough to cause it to be abandoned and the boat is returning to the relief vessel. The cast iron legs of the circular barrack used by the men who built Dubh Artach were left on the rock after its completion in 1872 and show up exceptionally well in this card.

DUBH ARTACH LIGHTHOUSE. (S.W. OF THE ISLE OF MULL.) B.6003.

Dhu. Heartach Lighthouse, West Coast of Scotland.
One of the most exposed rock stations in the United Kingdom. Tower is 126 feet high.
Stormy Weather at the Rock.

Left: This 1910 view of Dubh Artach is a good example of artistic embellishment of what is probably an original photograph. The 'Stormy Weather at the Rock' referred to on the card has been added afterwards to give a bit of drama to the scene. If it were possible to get a photograph of the lighthouse in really stormy weather it would probably look exactly like this, with waves up to the level of the lantern, but this is obviously the work of an artist who has added the 'storm and tempest' in the studio, not to mention the disturbed seabirds again!

The embossed border on a cream card that just shows up in this scan indicates that this card is one of a series published by the Lighthouse Literature Mission in Belfast. It was an organisation founded by Samuel H. Strain, in Belfast. His idea was to send free literature to the lighthouse keepers to entertain and educate them through their lonely hours. He also produced a series of stylish postcards with pictures of lighthouses and lightships from around the world that are now very much sought after by postcard collectors.

Right: A very skilful and realistic piece of artistic enhancement of Bishop Rock lighthouse when a real photograph was obviously out of the question! When waves travel over 3,000 miles across the Atlantic Ocean backed by a howling gale, the Isles of Scilly are the first bit of Britain they reach, and the Bishop Rock lighthouse is the first bit of the Isles of Scilly they thump into – with spectacular effect. Dark skies, water up to the lantern gallery and the sea a boiling mass of white water. It's even too rough for the seabirds to make an appearance in this card.

BISHOP ROCK LIGHTHOUSE
IN A HOWLING GALE   E 35

Left and right: This one isn't quite so realistic. The waves have been added to an original photograph of the Eddystone to give the impression of stormy seas breaking over the reef, but there's something in the finished card that doesn't look quite right.

And when you compare it to the photograph on the right that it was based on you can see why. It's actually a relief day at the Eddystone but the cluster of keepers on the set-off and the relief vessel beyond have all be disguised behind crashing waves which have also been added to the reef in the foreground. The flagpole on the gallery with a limp flag (because there's no wind) has been removed in the 'rough seas' version, but the two giant fog bells remain.

Right: I can't make up my mind about this card – is it real, or has a photograph taken in calm weather been embellished? It's a true enough representation of the kind of scenes that could occur at Wolf Rock in times of storm, but the water in the foreground looks comparatively calm compared to the tumult going on around the lighthouse.

365. The Wolf Rock Lighthouse, during a storm.   Gibson Penzance.

THE EDDYSTONE LIGHTHOUSE.

10·9·03

Dear S.—
I hope you are enjoying yourself this fine(?) weather. How are you getting along with P.—? Same as usual? I would very much like to hear some news. Did you have an opportunity of sending that P.P.C. of Micawber.— Please tell M.— the S.— are not mine. Don't laugh.— Much love Jessie

Raphael Tuck & Sons' "Rough Sea" Postcard. Series 148.
Phototyped in Saxony

Left: Compare this card with the one on the title page of this chapter – there's an unmistakable similarity of content. One of the artists, or perhaps it's even the same one, has used one card as the basis for another, even down to the positioning of the ship and groups of seabirds. The earlier card was dated at 1904 and the writer of this card has very conveniently dated it quite accurately for us – 10th September 1903, which probably means the similarity of design is no coincidence. This card shows the Douglass lighthouse that is only 21 years old. It's from a "Rough Sea" series and contains some intriguing correspondence from someone called Jessie.

Notice that all the correspondence has been squeezed into what little free space there is around the image. The Post Office allowed only the address to be written on the backs of early postcards. However, from around September 1903 onwards, it allowed a message to be written on the left-hand side of the back and the recipient's address to be written on the right-hand side. To accommodate this, the card publishers started to produce postcards with a line down the middle of the card – the divided back that we have today. However the old stocks of cards with undivided backs were still being posted in large numbers between 1902 and 1904. And this is a fine example.

Right: Quite a nice sepia card showing much the same as the previous card, except that this one is looking east because (a slightly exaggerated) Smeaton's stump is to the right of the present tower. But the birds are still looking for a safe roost and a tall ship battles its way through the storm in the background. Strangely, the artist has drawn the lighthouse as if it were expecting a relief – a flag is flying from the lantern and the handrails around the set-off have been rigged – but we can obviously see that such a thing would be impossible in these conditions.

THE EDDYSTONE LIGHTHOUSE.

5 CURIOSITIES

Above: This is something that shouldn't really happen! A tramp steamer, the *Blue Jacket*, is stuck fast on the Longships reef – directly below the lighthouse that was flashing its warning about the very reef the ship ploughed on to. It happened in December 1898 when the *Blue Jacket* was steaming from Plymouth to Cardiff. The captain went below to his cabin at 9.30pm but was woken at midnight as his vessel shuddered to a stop on the Longships. On a now listing deck he found the whole shambolic scene being brilliantly illuminated by the lighthouse. Quite how the mate on watch managed to wedge the ship in this position with over two miles of visibility has never been explained. The *Blue Jacket* remained in this embarrassing position for over a year!

This final chapter contains postcards I've come across in the course of researching this book, that don't readily fall into one of the other chapters. There is something interesting, unique or unusual about the image they display. The card itself might be particularly rare and no such equivalent exists today. Or it might show a scene that would be impossible to view again – a lighthouse being built or dismantled, or a lighthouse that no longer exists for instance. Some of them don't feature a lighthouse at all, but something connected with it that was deemed worthy of a postcard up to a century ago.

Some of the lighthouses will have appeared in preceding chapters, but there are some that are new to these pages. Most of the cards represent what we would call social history – nostalgic scenes from the past showing how things used to be.

Right: There were no such things as postcards when this lighthouse existed, but this is a painting that has been turned into a postcard. It was done by Victor Hugo and shows Henry Winstanley's second Eddystone tower of 1699. This was a modification of his first tower of 1698 – the first lighthouse ever to be built on a wave-swept rock anywhere in the world. Illuminated by tallow candles that were only 35 feet above high water, winter gales passed over it so its dimensions were increased, making it taller and wider. Winstanley was so confident in his modified design that he declared he could wish for nothing better than to be in it during 'the greatest storm that ever was'. It lasted for a few years, but the elaborate and fanciful design was eventually its downfall. 'The Great Storm' of November 1703 swept it from the reef and took its builder, who was inside at the time, with it. Winstanley got his wish.

24 - MAISON DE VICTOR-HUGO (Musée) - Le Phare d'Eddystone
« L'Homme qui Rit », dessin de Victor Hugo

Left: The Nab tower was built towards the end of World War I in great secrecy. It was originally intended to be one of a chain of towers with submarine nets stretched between them, but with the end of hostilities it was used to replace the Nab lightvessel in the Solent.

This hand-tinted card from about 1917–18 shows an almost complete Nab tower in Southwick harbour on the Sussex coast. Interestingly, the caption to the card refers to a 'lighthouse' – which is the obvious stone tower in the foreground. But the giant concrete structure in the background that would also become a lighthouse, was described as a 'Tower Ship' – such was the mystery that surrounded its construction and purpose.

Right: This card even calls the huge structure a 'mystery tower'. It gives us a good view of its construction, mainly the massive concrete base that sits on the bed of The Solent supporting a metal superstructure. On its flat top we can see a smaller circular structure in the centre. This would turn out to be the lantern of the Nab light. You can see what it looks like in its final position in Chapter 1. In this view the tower is described as being in Shoreham harbour, which is basically the same inlet of water as Southwick harbour.

The Wreuah Series. No. 1512

Beachy Head.

Left: Postcards of lighthouses being built, particularly at remote locations, are not common, but they do exist – like this card showing the new tower at the base of Beachy Head cliffs under construction. The new lighthouse was sited just 530ft from the base of the cliffs which meant an aerial ropeway could be used to deliver the workforce and their materials from the top of the cliff.

This black and white card shows the wooden framework that serves as the upper landing on the cliff top. We can just see the faint outline of the wire rope descending to the metal-legged platform at the other end. On it was a crane that made the final delivery of granite blocks to the masons inside the growing tower.

Attached to the wire rope was a crude open cable car that carried everything needed down to the work site. This included the workforce who would make the very exposed trip twice a day. Our modern Health and Safety Executive would have apoplexy if they saw some of the photographs of this delivery service in action!

The tower and landing stage look all but complete in this view – only the lantern remains to be fitted, which means it probably dates from 1901.

Right: Down at sea level and the tide is in. The lantern is in place and the lighthouse is almost complete. The black band (its original colour) is being painted by someone suspended in a cradle from the lantern gallery, and the crane is still on the landing stage. It's probably only a matter of weeks before the lighthouse becomes operational in October 1902.

New Beachy Head Lighthouse   Eastbourne

Stengel & Co., London E. C. 39 Redcross Street 14766

EDDYSTONE LIGHTHOUSE, PLYMOUTH.

Left and right: Two identical cards posted three years apart. They both show an even rarer event than a lighthouse being built – a lighthouse being dismantled. In this case it's Smeaton's tower on the Eddystone, and it is already nearly down to the stump that remains today. We can see the silhouettes of people working on the old lighthouse and the vessel that was taking the blocks back to Plymouth is standing off in the background.

The black and white version was posted in 1911 which meant that the image was already 29 years old, as the dismantling of the tower was done in 1882 when the new Douglass tower was finished. The colour version was posted even later, in 1914, but curiously the weather vane and the flag that are so obvious in the first version have disappeared in the coloured version.

Eddystone Lighthouse, Plymouth.

Right: Postcards that didn't show the lighthouse itself, but some of the peripheral buildings were popular with the keepers and their families as a means of keeping in touch with their relatives and friends posted elsewhere. The rather functional and austere stone architecture of the keepers' accommodation at Rattray Head lighthouse, between Peterhead and Fraserburgh, is typical of several Northern Lighthouse Board stations.

Rattray Head lighthouse, as we shall see later in this chapter, is technically a pillar light so the keepers' families lived on shore in this very solid looking block. The actual lighthouse is visible to the left of the accommodation. The photographer has managed to persuade two men and two boys (and their dog) to pose outside the 'cottage' with the open door. The card was posted in 1914.

Lighthouse Keepers' House, Rattray.   Gammie, Photo.

"Flugga Lighthouse, Shore, Station, Burrafirth, Unst."

Photo J.D.Rattar

Left: The architecture at this NLB shore station is undeniably similar to the one at Rattray Head – a solid, square block with a flat roof and tall chimneys. But this is 250 miles further north, almost as far north as it is possible to get in the British Isles. This is the shore station built in 1855 for Muckle Flugga lighthouse located in an inlet called Burra Firth on the island of North Unst in the Shetlands. It is where the keepers who were stationed at Muckle Flugga would return after their turn of duty at a lighthouse that was nearer to the Artic Circle than it was to London, and nearer to Bergen in Norway than Edinburgh in Scotland!

This structure was one of the most northerly permanently inhabited buildings in Britain. It's sited on a mound of land overlooking Burra Firth at the end of the road from Haroldswick, a tiny village on North Unst. To get to Lerwick – the main town of Shetland – involves a 60-mile drive involving two ferries that takes about 2½ hours. But to get to Muckle Flugga lighthouse was a 6½ mile sea trip down the Firth and across to Muckle Flugga – a much easier journey. The unidentified vessel in the background of this card could be an NLB tender waiting to change the keepers.

Since the lighthouse was automated in 1995, the keepers have moved out and the building has been converted into the Hermaness Visitor Centre.

Right: Another of those 'who would want to buy a postcard of this scene' cards. There must have been a market for it to have been produced. Flat Holm, in the Bristol Channel, was not always devoid of permanent residents as it is today, but was the site of a former cholera hospital and many military installations from different wars. It was a popular destination for day trips from South Wales, so perhaps a souvenir of the impressive foghorns would be a postcard of them.

We're looking at another rather architecturally uninspiring piece of lighthouse periphery in the form of the foghorn building on the island. While the bricks and mortar may be purely functional in their design the two giant foghorns projecting from its roof certainly look as if they could produce a substantial noise.

It was built in 1908, together with a foghorn keeper's cottage, about half a mile from the lighthouse itself. The siren was originally powered by a 15hp diesel engine, which gave two blasts in quick succession at two-minute intervals that could be clearly heard by people living on the Welsh and Somerset coasts. Volunteers from the Flat Holm Society, with help from the Princes Trust, restored the horn and engines in the 1960s and the house is now a Listed Building. The Foghorn Station was officially reopened by Secretary of State for Wales and the First Minister for Wales in May 2000 when the foghorn was sounded for the first time since 1988.

This card was posted in 1918 and we can already see what look like cracks appearing in the structure that have been filled and repaired, a result of the huge vibrations that this monster would have produced perhaps? One of the keepers poses proudly at the door of the building, but he would probably have been equally proud of the vegetable garden in front of him. We can see neat rows of vegetables already planted and a row of sticks that would probably support a crop of peas when they were big enough.

The Fog Horn. Flat Holm.

La Corbiere, Jersey

Left: It's certainly one of Jersey's most iconic landmarks and frequently appears in publicity material to entice visitors to the island, but La Corbière ('gathering place of the crows') lighthouse has another claim to fame. It was the first British lighthouse to be built entirely from reinforced concrete.

Designed by Sir John Coode and completed in 1874, the lighthouse marks a reef extending half a mile into the sea from the south-western corner of Jersey. At high tide the lighthouse is cut off – as the lower card from 1902 shows clearly. But at low water it can be reached on a causeway that is visible in the upper card from 1959. It's a dangerous place, both for shipping heading in and out of St Helier, and also for its many visitors. A plaque at one end of the causeway commemorates keeper Peter Larbalestier who was drowned in May 1946 trying to rescue a holidaymaker caught out by the tide.

The attractive white tower is only 62ft high, but being perched on the highest pinnacle of the reef gives it a height of 119ft above high water. Using concrete to build it made the use of stonemasons to cut, shape and dovetail granite blocks together unnecessary. The total cost for the lighthouse, its keeper's cottage and the causeway was only £8000!

Initially it used paraffin vapour to produce its flash, but in 1976 it was electrified and automated at the same time, although the original fittings and mechanisms are still in pristine condition. In fact the whole tower, now over 130 years old, has suffered very little at the hands of the sea that often passes completely over it in times of storm. It is said that because it is made of concrete and therefore has a smooth continuous outer skin, there are no joints between blocks that the sea could erode and force its way into.

Even though Trinity House looks after most of the major lights in the Channel Islands, La Corbière is maintained by the Jersey Harbour Authority. Both of these views show the lighthouse and its exposed and rugged location extremely well. The writer of the bottom card hopes ' . . . you are as well as we feel'.

99   JERSEY. — Corbiere Lightouse — Le Phare de la Corbiére.
LL

Above and right: Close up, La Corbière lighthouse looks like this. The causeway leads to an impressive flight of steps up to the tower. These cards show groups of men and women scattered all around the lighthouse and on the steps, but it also gives a good idea as to the rugged nature of the reef and why the light was needed. The tower appears to be built of blocks, but these are just grooves carved out of the concrete to give the impression of courses of granite.

The right-hand card carries the intials LL in the bottom right hand corner. This indicates it was photographed by Louis (sometimes referred to as Lucien) Levy – a French photographer and postcard publisher who is noted for producing high quality postcards of British, French and even North African scenes that display interesting compositions and superb detail. He seemed to have a fascination for ports, docks and harbours and the ships that used them so his study of La Corbière lighthouse is not unexpected.

Copyright, E. O. CATFORD, Guernsey.

Platte Fougère Lighthouse, Guernsey

Left: We remain in the Channel Islands for this next light, one of the most unusual and unique British lighthouses, but it's one that few people not familiar with the waters around Guernsey have even heard of.

There are many features that make Platte Fourgère of interest to lighthouse enthusiasts; firstly it's constructed from concrete, secondly it was Britain's first remotely-controlled lighthouse, and lastly its construction was the result of a suggestion from no less an authority than David and Charles Stevenson – the great Scottish lighthouse engineers.

The main approach to St Peter Port harbour on Guernsey was partly obstructed by reefs such as the Grand Braye and Platte Fourgère upon which countless vessels came to grief. The merchants and shipowners petitioned the Guernsey Parliament for some kind of warning device so General Campbell, who was the Governor General of Guernsey at the time, approached David and Charles Stevenson. A huge pillar light in the style of Eddystone or Skerryvore was financially out of the question for the island, so after surveying the reefs they suggested an automatic light and fog signal on Platte Fourgère, controlled by a submarine cable from the mainland.

This card shows what they produced. While not an elegant light it was certainly functional and it 'only' cost £10,000. The solid base of the 83ft tower was formed from Portland cement poured into iron moulds, although much of the foundations for the tower were under water and could only be worked on at low tide. Above this were two rooms, the first contained electric motors and the foghorn compressor, and the one above it housed the back-up equipment. Large compressed air storage tanks are visible at the top of the tower next to the fog siren. It became operational on 15th March 1910

There's no lantern as such – just an automatic 17,600 candlepower flashing beacon that is now electric, but was originally powered by acetylene which had to be delivered by boat at regular intervals. It was all controlled from Fort Doyle on Guernsey.

Right: This view is from the other side of the tower to the other card, and we can see a bit more detail of this unusual lighthouse. It's obviously low tide because the reef is partly visible, and the sea is calm enough to allow a boat to tie up at its base. This is probably a delivery of acetylene for the lantern.

The solid base extends for 46ft up to the platform by the entrance door and to get there meant climbing the very obvious vertical ladder. We can see the windows of the two rooms, and above these on its 'roof' is its self-contained automatic lantern, and the large compressed air tanks that drove the foghorn known locally as 'The Lowing Cow'. This was said to be powerful enough to be heard in France.

In recent years the concrete base between high and low water has suffered much erosion from nearly a century of wave bombardment. It may have survived two World Wars but the sea had single-handedly eroded its walls, leaving it in urgent need of repair. A waterproof and weatherproof mortar was applied by men dangling from cradles in the summer of 1997.

One particular accolade awarded to this light, which I haven't mentioned so far, is that it's often described as the ugliest lighthouse in the world, and looking at it in this card you might agree. In its defence I should say that it's had a bit of a facelift since this picture was taken, and the bare concrete has been painted brilliant white with a broad black band around its midriff.

PLATTE FOUGÈRE LIGHTHOUSE,

GUERNSEY.   (COPYRIGHT.)

Lighthouse Bass Rock

Left: Lighthouse sundials north of the border were commonplace items and almost every lighthouse had one. They were all of a standard design – a bollard-like cast-iron plinth with a fluted shaft mounted on a square stone base.

They were a vital piece of lighthouse equipment because it was an NLB requirement that at regular intervals, and at least once per week, the Principal Keeper should check the lighthouse timepiece against the sundial. If the sundial had been correctly positioned the lighthouse clock could be relied upon to be accurate when keeping the records of weather conditions, passing shipping and even shipwrecks.

The instructions for 'calibrating' the sundial with the clock said that when the sun is shining the lighthouse keeper should wait for the shadow to coincide with an hour or half hour mark, then set the lighthouse clock to match. Subsequently, the keeper was to make a further adjustment of any minutes required for the time of year, from an equation engraved on the dial. Sundial adjustment became unnecessary when BBC radio time signals – the pips – started.

This 1905 card shows the sundial at Bass Rock lighthouse, with someone we presume could be a keeper posing in his civvies alongside. It doesn't look a particularly sunny day so it's unlikely he is checking the accuracy of the lighthouse clock.

Right and Below: Another lighthouse not built from traditional stone is found here at Whitford Point (sometimes 'Whiteford') at the entrance to the River Loughor estuary, north of the Gower peninsula in South Wales.

There's quite a bit of fine detail on the sepia card; we can see that it has a traditional oak-tree outline very similar to Smeaton's Eddystone, and two galleries – one around the white lantern and one lower down. What is also clear is that it's constructed entirely from cast-iron plates bolted together – no granite, no concrete just cast iron. It also still appears to be a working lighthouse, unlike the 1934 card below where it has sadly suffered much torment from the weather and the waves.

It replaced an earlier wooden structure from 1854 that was so badly damaged by storm the following year it was abandoned. After repairs, it was reinstated in 1857, then struck by a ship and damaged again! By 1864 the Llanelli Harbour Trust had had enough and commissioned local engineer John Bowen to build them another light 300 yards to the south of this one.

He was the designer of the tapering cast-iron tower we see in these cards, first operational in November 1866. By 1919 it was an automatic light powered by acetylene, but suffered greatly from the cast-iron plates either working loose or cracking. In the five years between 1880 and 1885 over 150 metal hoops were reported to have been placed around the tower to stabilise it. Concrete blocks were laid around its base in 1886 to prevent the erosion of the soft sand on which it was built.

In 1921 another light was built by the Harbour Trust at Burry Holms to the south west, and in 1926 it was decided to discontinue Whitford Point light. It still exists today, Britain's only offshore cast-iron lighthouse, and can be visited at low water with great care and a long walk over soft sands with a final rocky approach – like the man in the card with his two dogs has done. It survived being used for bomb practice during World War II and has been a listed monument since 1979. Interestingly in 2000 it was put up for sale for £1 (despite estimated restoration costs of £100,000) and attracted worldwide interest, including an American millionaire who wanted to dismantle and ship the lighthouse to America.

WHITFORD LIGHTHOUSE. LLANGENNITH SANDS.

WHITFORD, LIGHT-HOUSE LLANMADOCK. A.V. 1398.

Wyre Light   Fleetwood

*bbott Series.

Left: The Wyre lighthouse (originally known as Port Fleetwood light) marked a significant development of lighthouse engineering, but has sadly been allowed to fall into dereliction and decay. The structure you see in this 1909 card still exists in a deplorable state, and needless to say it's no longer a functioning light.

It was the first screw pile lighthouse in the world, and the prototype of a design that was copied worldwide for lighthouses in certain locations where solid foundations didn't exist. Built in 1840 by Alexander Mitchell, a blind Irish engineer, it consists of 7 screw piles sunk into the seabed at the northern edge of North Wharf, the sandbank stretching seaward for 2 miles from Fleetwood towards Lune Deeps in Morecambe Bay.

Each pile was 16ft long and had a cast-iron screw base 3ft in diameter. The six corner piles formed a hexagonal platform 50ft in diameter with the seventh pile acting as a centre pillar. The platform supported a two-storey wooden building to house the keepers, with the lantern on top of this. Construction began in 1839 and the light was first lit on 6th June 1840.

Its original colour was red, but after the schooner *Elizabeth and Jane* rammed it in 1870, this was changed to black to make it a little more obvious! It's possible, but difficult to tell in a sepia card, that this could be its original red colour.

It survived a century of storms before a disastrous fire destroyed it in 1948. Sadly it was not rebuilt but converted to automatic operation and eventually replaced by a lighted buoy in 1979. The legs are still there but little else – a sad end for a remarkable piece of early Victorian engineering.

This view could have been taken by a photographer who walked to the lighthouse, took his picture and walked back to Fleetwood. It shows clearly the arrangement of metal legs and their bracing, together with the wooden accommodation and lantern. There's a keeper on the gallery and a wooden rowing boat suspended lifeboat-style from davits. To the left of the lantern is what appears to be a curious signalling system consisting of a white post supporting two horizontal arms – in a very similar design to something that might be used on a railway. It would be visible through a telescope from Fleetwood, so it was perhaps some kind of semaphore device.

Right: This is a lovely sepia card that is much sought after by postcard collectors because it just captures perfectly a moment in time that has gone forever. True social history.

It's high tide this time at the Wyre light, and a steamer has arrived to either change the keepers or deliver stores. The rowing boat in the water has come from the steamer as the lighthouse boat is still in place on the gallery with someone standing in it. They're not very clear but there are another four men in this card, one on the gallery just to the left of the entrance 'porch', and three on a lower platform beneath it.

There's so much interesting detail to be seen – the horn of the foghorn sticking out of the roof, the even taller kitchen chimney, a large bell in its own frame, and the lantern itself with wind vane and its curtains drawn so the sun didn't damage the lamps inside. There's a large black tank on the roof of the keepers' quarters which is probably used for storing rainwater, and the steamer standing off continues to belch black smoke even though it's not moving.

If you saw the state this historic light is in today you'd be appalled.

1127   WYRE LIGHT FLEETWOOD CHANNEL.

Rattray Head Lighthouse, Scotland, East Coast.
Tower, 113 feet high.

Left: We've already seen the substantial accommodation for the keepers at this light earlier in the chapter, but this is the actual light they attended. It's quite a quirky design, and one that made it notable for two things. It was the first rock lighthouse to have a substantial fog siren installed, and secondly it was the only rock lighthouse to have been relieved by tractor!

Rattray Head was built to warn ships off a notorious reef called Rattray Briggs a short distance from the extensive sand dunes of this part of the Buchan coast. David Stevenson was the engineer and he planned an innovative new design – a tower built on Ron Rock in two parts, the lower containing a foghorn and engine-room, while the upper housed the lightkeepers' room and lantern.

Work was begun in 1892, and the masonry of both portions of the tower was completed in sixteen months. The lower granite section contained 20,000 cubic feet of dressed granite blocks, was 46ft high, with an entrance door reached by a 32ft outside ladder. At high water it was covered to within 7ft of the door but it was possible to walk ashore when the tide was out. The upper tower, had a diameter of 21ft for the lightroom, lantern and dome giving a total height of 120ft above the rock. The engine-room was at the entrance level, and the upper tower and siren all rise from a platform known colloquially as the 'quarter deck'. The light was exhibited for the first time on 14th October 1895.

During World War II the enemy aircraft that caused much panic at lights in the northern isles arrived at Rattray Head on 20th September 1941. One of them circled the lighthouse, dropped three bombs, only two of which exploded. The lantern was machine-gunned but the damage caused did not seriously impair the efficiency of the apparatus. Fortunately, no one was injured in the attack.

A mains electricity supply and telephone cable were laid under the seabed in September 1977 that meant the station could be electrified. In February 1982, the light was made fully automatic and the keepers withdrawn. Until they left their reliefs were accomplished by tractor at low water, and sometimes in darkness if this coincided with low water.

The view in this 1913 card shows the solid base with its entrance doors open.

Right: It was not unusual for the keepers at remote lighthouses to receive occasional visits from gentlemen of the cloth to offer spiritual, moral or practical advice to the keepers – if needed. All rock lighthouses were officially assigned to a parish and therefore the keepers were parishioners of a particular church. The more adventurous clergy were often dedicated in their duty to meet with all their parishioners and it wasn't unusual to find them being hauled inside some of our remotest pillar lights.

Such a visit has just happened in this card of an unknown chaplain returning from Bishop Rock which is visible in the background. He looks none the worse for his ordeal on the end of a rope. The unknown man on the far left with the cap and waders could possibly be a keeper who has been changed at the same time.

PENMON LIGHTHOUSE AND PUFFIN ISLAND.

Left: The easternmost point of the island of Anglesey in North Wales is a small humped rock called Puffin Island or Ynys Seiriol. The channel between it and Anglesey is less than a mile wide – just passable with care and a reasonable tide. The channel hides shingle banks and rocks barely visible until low water. The greatest danger lies at a spot called Black Point or Trwyn Du.

The Liverpool master pilots had already been consulted about the necessity for a light on the shore at this location but no action was taken until 1838 when Trinity House's engineer James Walker built his first rock lighthouse here at a cost of £11,589. The 96ft white tower with three black bands and a castellated lantern gallery is situated on a half-submerged rock surrounded by shingle beaches about half a mile south of Puffin Island. It has the characteristic stepped base that Walker featured on several of the lights he later designed such as The Smalls and Wolf Rock.

Although it was officially a pillar light it must have been the only one where its keepers could walk to work! It was connected by an iron walkway from the beach. The remains of it are clearly visible in this card which is dated 1933, eleven years after it had been automated and its keepers withdrawn.

This sepia card refers to the lighthouse by its alternative name of Penmon and behind it we can see the rugged profile of Puffin Island and the narrow channel that separates the light from mainland Anglesey.

Right: A slightly different angle in this early 1901 hand-tinted card, but the iron walkway to the tower is still obvious. The two keepers of the lighthouse lived in the cottages on the right. However these were withdrawn in 1922 when the lighthouse was converted to unwatched acetylene operation at the same time as another Welsh light at St Tudwal's that we have already come across in Chapter 2.

We can also see the triangular beacon in the channel to the right of the Puffin Island. This marks Perch Rock. Notice also there is the hint of black writing on the left side of the lighthouse. There aren't many British lighthouses that offer written instructions to passing mariners but Trwyn Du carries the very definite warning of 'No Passage Landward'.

The lighthouse was converted to solar power in 1996 when a bank of solar panels was installed on its gallery. Further work to modernise the station included the development of a unique operating mechanism to toll the 178kg working fog bell.

Puffin Island, Beaumaris

122   Landing at Round Island. Scilly.   Gibson Penzance

Left: This is the same landing at Round Island that we saw in Chapter 3, but in slightly calmer conditions. What's interesting here is that the people being landed are not keepers but visitors. There's clearly a lady in a long crinoline dress being helped up the vertical steps out of the boat, while just above her are a couple of other people in sleeves and hats. I mentioned earlier in the book that Round Island was a popular place for a daytrip, and this is the only place where you could get on to the island.

Right: And when they all reached the summit of the island outside the lighthouse, it was time for another photograph. This is probably the same group as in the last photograph and we can now see that the ones in sleeves and hats climbing the near vertical ladder are, in fact, ladies. I think that the small group to the right of the photo in front of the foghorn station contains three, if not four of the Round Island keepers. Whatever the reason for the visit, it was certainly important enough to require smart clothing and hats to be worn!

Round Island Lighthouse. Scilly   Gibson Penzance

Start Point Lighthouse, Sanday, Orkney.

Reit's Viking Series

"Do you ken this place"

Left: With a couple of notable exceptions such as Ardnamurchan and the Butt of Lewis, most of the older Scottish lighthouses are painted white to increase their visibility as daymarks. But this hasn't always been the case. For many years they were left 'as built' and it was possible to see exactly what they were built from – usually granite blocks or bricks.

Here's an excellent card showing just that. This is Start Point on the Orkney island of Sanday, not to be confused with Trinity House's Start Point in Devon. It clearly shows that it, and the keepers' house, were built from bricks and quite a considerable number of them. The NLB's Chief Engineer, the famous Robert Stevenson, built the 81ft tower in 1806, a year before he started his great work on the Bell Rock. It was the first Scottish lighthouse to have a revolving light which gave it a unique character making it easily distinguishable from other lights.

What is particularly interesting about this card, if you haven't already spotted it, is the postmark – San Bernardino, California, October 21st 1907. This isn't where it was posted, but where it was delivered to. On the reverse is a red One Penny stamp bearing the head of King Edward VII and postmarked Sanday, Kirkwall, October 7th 1907. It took this card just 14 days to cross the Atlantic and then America, and the only correspondence it carried (apart from the address) were the words "Do you ken this place" on the right-hand side of the card! It has since travelled all the way back to the UK because it now sits in my collection of lighthouse cards. A world record for the greatest number of miles travelled by a postcard perhaps?

Right: Compare this with the previous view of Start Point. It's the same lighthouse and keepers' house but they've been painted in a very striking and unique colour scheme. Although there are several lighthouses around our coasts painted white with black bands, or even completely black with a white lantern, there's no other British lighthouse that bears vertical black and white stripes.

Its unique colouring has often been likened to a St Mirren football club shirt, or even more dramatically – to a Polaris missile!

As to the date, difficult to tell with any great accuracy, except that it must be after 1915 as this is when its stripes were added.

START LIGHTHOUSE, SANDAY 364/1

New Brighton Lighthouse

Left: If you didn't know differently, you'd imagine that this impressive looking 90ft pillar light, that bears more than a passing resemblance to Smeaton's Eddystone, was built on a rock miles from an exposed headland around our coast. Sadly that's not the case. New Brighton is the point where the River Mersey empties into Liverpool Bay on the opposite side of the river to Liverpool itself, and this lighthouse is known as Perch Rock. It was built between 1827–30 out of 'marble rock' from Anglesey and lasted as a navigational aid until October 1973. Its base is all solid dovetailed blocks for the first 45ft to the entrance door and above that it had all the different rooms you would associate with a rock lighthouse. In recent times it's even been refurbished and marketed as a venue for newly-married couples to spend their honeymoon night. It came complete with a television in case they got bored with looking at the sea!

This 1905 card shows a paddle steamer heading west towards the Irish Sea, and in the distance the smoke from another vessel obscures the miles upon miles of Liverpool docks. It was still operational at this time and so the fog bell hanging from the gallery was frequently used.

Lighthouse, Low Tide, New Brighton.

Left: When the tide goes out you get a different perspective of Perch Rock! It's close enough to the shore to walk to, as hundreds of people did at every opportunity. This card must surely hold some kind of record for the number of people in the same card. Try and count them – it's impossible! But they all seem to be having an enjoyable time, either examining the rock pools or just taking the sea air.

The lighthouse details are even clearer. Notice how at the top of the tower the masonry forms a cornice to deflect waves away from the lantern. The gallery railings have an interesting bellied style that mirrors the masonry below them, and we can see that there are in fact two fog bells hanging from the gallery. Inside the lantern, the curtains are drawn to prevent sun damage, and to the left of the entrance ladder is the conduit that could be carrying the electric cable from the mainland. Altogether a very interesting card full of history, fashion and architecture from a century ago. Today, the tower has been painted white and is topped by a red lantern, but it's also floodlit at night.

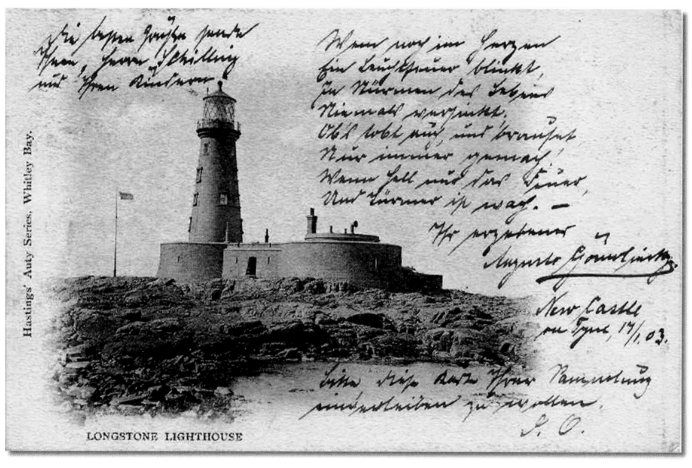

Hastings' Auty Series, Whitley Bay.

LONGSTONE LIGHTHOUSE

Left: Here's a puzzle for German speakers – what on earth is this card about? When it was written in 1903 all correspondence had to be written on the front of the card – its reverse was for the address only. The German author has certainly squeezed a great deal of news onto its face completely encircling the image of Longstone lighthouse that has not yet acquired a white band around its tower. The only words that are legible are the author's Christian name – Auguste – who wrote his card in Newcastle upon Tyne on 17th January 1903.

Right: I've mentioned on a couple of occasions how lighthouse keepers used postcards of their lighthouses to send to other keepers or their friends and families in order to keep in touch before the era of the telephone.

By way of a change, the last image in this book features the reverse of a postcard that was written in November 1913 and has been used for exactly this purpose. It's from a Mr J. Lockhart, who was a keeper at Sanda lighthouse, to Mr Williamson who was the principal keeper at Stoer Head lighthouse on the west coast (which he has mis-spelt as 'Stourhead'). The content is basic, but fascinating, chit-chat about health and the relocation of other Northern Lighthouse Board keepers. I have reproduced it in full because it gives an idea of the kind of use for which postcards were intended.

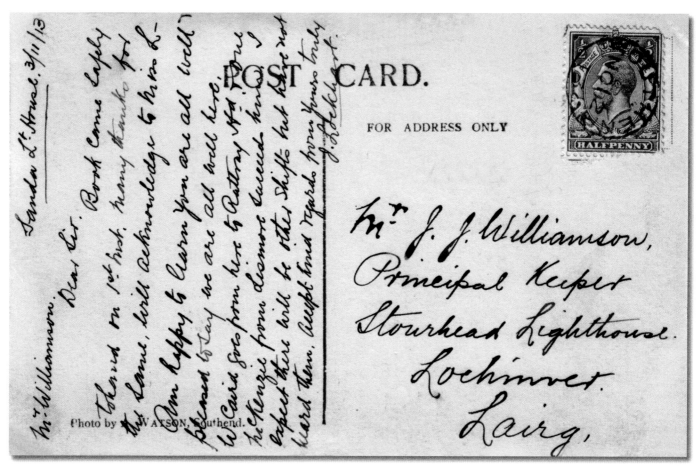

Mr Williamson   Sanda Lt.House 3/11/13
   Dear Sir,
Book came safely to hand on 1st. inst. Many thanks for the same. Will acknowledge to Miss L— Am happy to learn you are all well & pleased to say we are all well here. W. Caird goes from here to Rattray Hd. & one McKenzie from Lismore succeeds him. I expect there will be other shifts but have not heard them. Accept kind regards from Yours truly.
                              J.Lockhart